The Blender Python API

Precision 3D Modeling and Add-on Development

Chris Conlan

Apress®

The Blender Python API: Precision 3D Modeling and Add-on Development

Chris Conlan
Bethesda, Maryland
USA

ISBN-13 (pbk): 978-1-4842-2801-2   ISBN-13 (electronic): 978-1-4842-2802-9
DOI 10.1007/978-1-4842-2802-9

Library of Congress Control Number: 2017944928

Cover image designed by Freepik

Managing Director: Welmoed Spahr
Editorial Director: Todd Green
Acquisitions Editor: Susan McDermott
Development Editor: Laura Berendson
Technical Reviewer: Justin Mancusi
Coordinating Editor: Rita Fernando
Copy Editor: Kezia Endsley
Compositor: SPi Global
Indexer: SPi Global

Distributed to the book trade worldwide by Springer Science+Business Media New York, 233 Spring Street, 6th Floor, New York, NY 10013. Phone 1-800-SPRINGER, fax (201) 348-4505, e-mail orders-ny@springer-sbm.com, or visit www.springeronline.com. Apress Media, LLC is a California LLC and the sole member (owner) is Springer Science + Business Media Finance Inc (SSBM Finance Inc). SSBM Finance Inc is a **Delaware** corporation.

For information on translations, please e-mail rights@apress.com, or visit http://www.apress.com/rights-permissions.

Apress titles may be purchased in bulk for academic, corporate, or promotional use. eBook versions and licenses are also available for most titles. For more information, reference our Print and eBook Bulk Sales web page at http://www.apress.com/bulk-sales.

Any source code or other supplementary material referenced by the author in this book is available to readers on GitHub via the book's product page, located at www.apress.com/9781484228012. For more detailed information, please visit http://www.apress.com/source-code.

Printed on acid-free paper

For my teachers and colleagues at the University of Virginia Department of Statistics.

Contents at a Glance

Contents at a Glance

Contents

About the Author

Chris Conlan began his career as an independent data scientist specializing in trading algorithms. He obtained his degree in statistics from the University of Virginia where he established himself as an expert in automated trading. His passion for intuitive data visualization introduced him to various 3D modeling and virtual reality suites that he hopes to better integrate into the lives of data scientists. He is currently managing development of private technology companies in high-frequency Forex, machine vision, and precision 3D modeling.

About the Technical Reviewer

Justin Mancusi attended the University of Virginia, where he obtained degrees in computer science and mathematics. In the past, he has worked as an independent consultant at the intersection of computing and statistics. He is experienced in a breadth of computational topics including advanced optimization, computational statistics, and stochastic processes.

Introduction

This text details the development and use of 3D modeling tools in Blender's Python API. We challenge the perception of Blender as purely an artist's tool by building precise data-driven models. Simultaneously, we teach you how aid and enable artists by deploying custom tools in the familiar Blender environment.

The knowledge presented in this text is the result of a deep understanding of not only Blender's documentation and source code, but also of the source code of add-ons written by Blender's core developers. The author has discovered many useful functionalities that are, as of the time of writing, undocumented. Thankfully, we as users can stay on the cutting edge by listening to and learning from those developers. This text unifies well-documented introductory material and undocumented advanced material to create a powerful reference.

This book is packed with code examples and screenshots of powerful scripts and add-ons. We include scripts to automate precise tasks that would otherwise be very difficult to implement by hand. In addition, we build add-ons that augment Blender's existing functionalities with new tools, objects, and customization options.

Definitions

3D modeling is the art of manipulating data to create 3D representations of objects and environments. 3D artists use the following tools and techniques to build 3D models.

- *Manual modeling* involves the artist interacting with a software interface. This can be:

  - Using a 3D modeling suite (Blender, Maya, or 3ds Max) to create and edit objects by hand

  - Playing video games with 3D building elements (Minecraft, Fallout 4, or Sims)

  - Manually inputting data into a 3D object file (.obj, .stl, or .glTF)

- *Automated Modeling* involves algorithmically generating 3D models. This can be:

  - Procedural generation of environments and characters in video games

  - Generating detailed models of buildings from architectural specifications

  - Producing 3D-printed art from fractal algorithms

- *Primitives* are the basic building blocks of 3D models. Though there are no strict rules on what constitutes a primitive, these can be:

  - Simple closed shapes like planes, cubes, and pyramids

  - Simple curved shapes like spheres, cylinders, and cones

  - Complex shapes like tori (plural of torus), Bezier curves, Nurbs surfaces

3D models are data representations of objects and environments. 3D models have the following components.

- *Data formats* allow models to differentiate and specialize by application. Every type of 3D model has a format by which it is specified. These include:

  - Suite-specific formats like .blend for Blender, .3ds for 3ds Max, and .ma for Maya

  - Renderer-specific formats like .babylon for BabylonJS, .json geometry descriptor for 3JS, and .glsl for OpenGL shaders

  - Minimalistic interchange formats like .obj and .stl

- *Vertices and faces* define the points and the surfaces connecting those points in 3D space.

  - Vertices are triplets of real numbers 3D space, or traditional (x, y, z) coordinates of each point of the object.

  - Faces are triplets of integers, where (i, j, k) represents the triangle in 3D space formed by the i-th, j-th, and k-th vertex.

Prerequisite Knowledge for This Book

This book covers Blender version 2.78c running Python 3.5.2. Most examples run on Blender 2.70 and greater, and the concepts apply to Blender generally. Nonetheless, it is recommended that readers use Blender 2.78c to best follow along. As we discuss the history and development of Blender and the Python language, we will point out programming practices that are not likely to work on past and future versions.

We assume a basic working knowledge of Blender and Python 3. Familiarity with any version of Blender 2.60 or greater is sufficient. Similarly, pure Python 2 programmers will have no problem following along.

Material Overview

This text introduces knowledge and sequentially builds on it to create more and more complete and complex software solutions. We introduce and discuss the following major topics.

Chapter 1: The Blender Interface

There are many individual interfaces that make up Blender. The core interfaces are highly scriptable because almost every possible user interaction is tied directly to a Python function. We establish some familiarity with those parts of the interface especially important for Python programming.

The Blender interface will act as both the deployment and development environment for your software. We discuss unique considerations for programming and testing Python while remaining in the Blender interface.

In an effort to minimize usage of screenshots throughout this text, we introduce important vocabulary for discussing the Blender interface. Using this vocabulary, we can focus on Python code while allowing users to work in their own preferred layout of the Blender interface.

Chapter 2: The bpy Module

The bpy module is the core of the Blender Python API. Learning to navigate this module will drastically improve your understanding both Blender and the API. Early in this book, we focus on classes within bpy that construct objects and manipulate their associated metadata. Later in the book, we access new classes in the bpy module that turn scripts into plugins.

The module itself is very verbose. Early scripts will appear both complicated and repetitive. After getting our feet wet with object creation and manipulation, we will begin adding useful function to a toolkit we will build throughout the book. We will store complex and commonly-used algorithms in the toolkit but encourage readers to commit core elements of the bpy module to memory. In this way, we create code that is both easy to write and easy to share.

Chapter 3: The bmesh Module

The bmesh module is a relatively new module that attempts to simplify complex vertex-level manipulation of object data. For those readers familiar with Blender, most of the operations in bmesh will only run in Edit Mode and not Object Mode. This serves to enforce that the functions in bmesh are for granular changes rather than global transformation of the mesh data.

This module, in the author's opinion, is what distinguishes the Blender Python API from other automated 3D modeling software. The bmesh module gives us algorithmic access to Blender's large suite of Edit Mode tools for vertex-level, edge-level, and face-level object manipulation. It allows us to write procedural generation algorithms for very complex objects in hundreds instead of thousands of lines of code.

Chapter 4: Topics in Modeling and Rendering

It is essential to anyone working in 3D modeling to have a basic understanding of the mechanisms we rely on to render and visualize our work product. We will discuss the basics of rendering pipelines and important rendering topics for Blender Python development. Many perceived bugs and strange behaviors in Blender and in visualizers to which we export are actually intended behaviors of renderers. We learn to detect and program around these behaviors to ensure we are creating highly portable models.

We discuss common and uncommon file formats, Z-fighting, normal vectors, the differences between software and hardware rendering, and much more. This will help us debug Python code based on behaviors we see in various rendering software.

Chapter 5: Introduction to Add-On Development

Bridging the gap between a script and a distributable add-on can be a difficult process that relies on very specific development practices, careful code organization, and occasional meta-programming. Many of these concepts mirror standard Python module development practices, while many others rely on unique behaviors of Blender's scripting interface.

We discuss GUI development, custom Blender data objects, bpy.types, and bpy.utils in detail here. We discuss organization of add-on files and ways to increase portability across different versions of Blender. At this point in the text, readers will be able to create add-ons that extend Blender to the benefit of modelers that do have Python experience.

Chapter 6: The bgl and blf Modules

The `bgl` module is an OpenGL wrapper for Blender that is useful for marking up, measuring, and visualizing objects and data in the Blender interface. The `blf` module is for drawing text and fonts with the Blender interface and is rarely used without the `bgl` module. We touch on the `bpy_extras` and `mathutils` modules to aid us here.

These modules are incredibly useful for add-on development, because we can influence the data the user sees without affecting the models themselves. We introduce them at this point in the text because their effectiveness depends on the ability to run them as add-ons.

Chapter 7: Advanced Add-On Development

Up to this point, we will have used Blender's Text Editor to create scripts and add-ons. The Text Editor introduces various limitations on the form of our add-ons that we overcome here. We also discuss best practices for data storage and module management by citing popular community add-ons. We conclude this chapter with a discussion of advanced GUI development.

Chapter 8: Textures and Rendering

Up to this point, we will have worked purely with meshes in Blender. In this chapter, we bring scenes to life with texturing and rendering. We discuss procedural *uv*-mapping, lighting placement, and camera positioning. With this discussion comes an overview of lighting types, camera perspective dynamics, and bounding box algorithms.

We conclude this chapter by procedurally rendering an arbitrary scene and providing a framework for automated rendering pipelines. We focus on still renderings in this chapter, but readers interested in automated animation will be able to extend the examples without difficulty.

History of Blender and Python

The relationship between the Blender interface and the Blender Python API is a rare one in the world of software development. It is typical for API-enabled platforms to treat users and developers as separate classes of citizens, complete with separate tools, separate environments, and separate goals. Blender, on the other hand, has erased the line between developers and users, making it easy for users to act as developers and vice versa.

The close relationship between developers and users is the product of wise early design decisions within Blender's core development team. Before Blender was released as free open source software in August 2003 as version 2.26, the core development team released the Python API documentation for the then-premium version 2.25. Python 2.0 had just been released in October 2000, and Blender was already using it to manage calls from the interface to its C-level data structures.

Released in 2009, Blender 2.50 and forward would use pure Python to dispatch editing tasks to its lower-level algorithms and data structures. Every action on the user interface was linked to a Python function, and the user had the option of accessing and calling these functions from consoles and scripts.

As we moved through the early 2010s, Blender artists would become increasingly aware of the influence Python scripting had on the modeling experience. Certain add-ons would become "must-haves" for artists with interests in certain fields. Developers of other 3D modeling software were jumping on the opportunity to develop exporters to port Blender to their software. Today, Blender has its modularity to thank for its massive talent pool, well-paying career opportunities, and active development community.

CHAPTER 1

■ ■ ■

The Blender Interface

This chapter discusses and defines components of Blender's interface. It serves as a reference for vocabulary we use to discuss the interface throughout the text. We will focus on components of the interface most often used in Python development, as well as set up custom interfaces for efficient Python scripting.

In an effort to avoid placing large screenshots throughout the book, we strictly define the names of various components in the Blender interface. Component names are introduced here in italics and appear with the first characters capitalized throughout the text.

The Default Blender Interface

When we first open up Blender, we get the familiar default user interface. We have a cube, a camera object, and a lamp object drawn into the scene shown in the *3D Viewport*. Figure 1-1 is a simple screenshot of the default Blender interface. Figure 1-2 shows the same interface with various major components labeled. We discuss the function of each of these interfaces.

■ **Note** We have applied the white-orange theme to our Blender interface for ease of printing. The default Blender theme is dark gray.

© Chris Conlan 2017

C. Conlan, *The Blender Python API*, DOI 10.1007/978-1-4842-2802-9_1

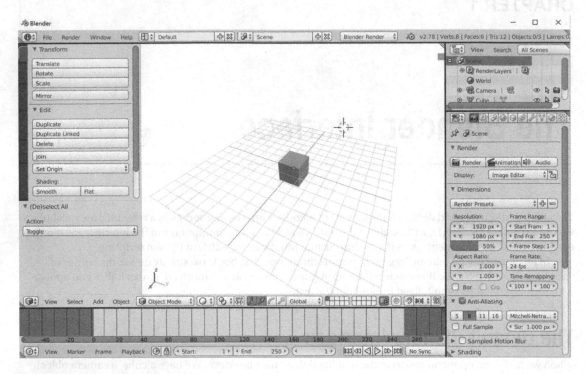

Figure 1-1. *The default Blender interface*

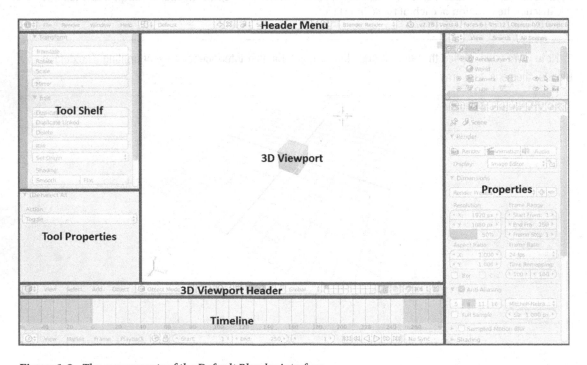

Figure 1-2. *The components of the Default Blender interface*

3D Viewport

The *3D Viewport,* or simply *Viewport,* gives us a preview of our work product. When we manipulate data in Blender, the 3D Viewport waits for all processes to finish writing data before updating itself. This is not noticeable in simple operations, like translations and rotations, that seem to happen instantaneously and in real time, but it is still important to acknowledge in add-on development.

The 3D Viewport has different viewing options and interaction options. Viewing options include *solid, wireframe,* and *rendered,* while interaction options include *Object Mode, Edit Mode,* and *Sculpt Mode.*

Header Menu

The *Header menu* is a fairly standard header for a graphical user interface. It allows us to switch between interface layouts like *Default, Animation,* and *Scripting,* as well as switch between rendering engines like *Blender Render, Cycles Render,* and *Blender Game.*

Properties Window

The *Properties* window allows us to access properties of objects, scenes, textures, animations, and more. Most interfaces in the Properties window will give summaries and basic attributes rather than display all available details. It is very useful for keeping track of existing objects, object names, applied and unapplied transformations, and a few other important attributes. This window is generally always open in a Blender artist's layout, so it is a popular location to place add-on functions.

Tool Shelf and Tool Properties

The *Tool Shelf* is where different classes of operators are grouped by type. If we expand the window, we can see the Tool Shelf has various tabs like *Tools, Create,* and *Relations.* Most Blender add-ons will create a new tab in the Tool Shelf to hold its operators and parameters.

The *Tool Properties* window is a dynamic window that Blender populates with different sets of parameters depending on what tool the user has active. For example, when using the Rotate tool, we can fine-tune the rotation in this window instead of navigating to the exact spot in the Properties window that specifies rotation. Tool Properties are advanced features typically intended to optimize ease-of-use rather than provide distinct functionalities to a tool. Many Blender add-ons ignore them altogether, and only a handful of native Blender tools use them.

Timeline

The *Timeline* is used in animation. We can ignore this as we will not be animating in this book.

The Scripting Interface

To enter the scripting interface, select the *Scripting* option in the drop-down menu to the right of the *Help* button within the Header menu. Throughout the text, we will present instructions like this with bold-faced directives, like: **Header Menu ➤ Screen Layout ➤ Scripting**. See Figure 1-3 for the location of the menu. The layout of Blender will change to appear like Figure 1-4.

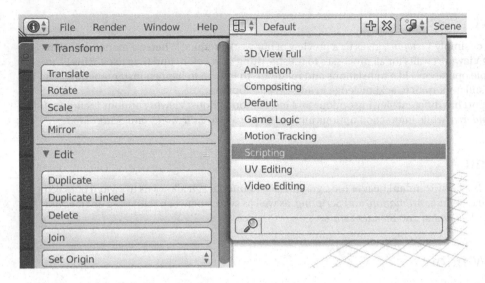

Figure 1-3. *Selecting the Scripting interface*

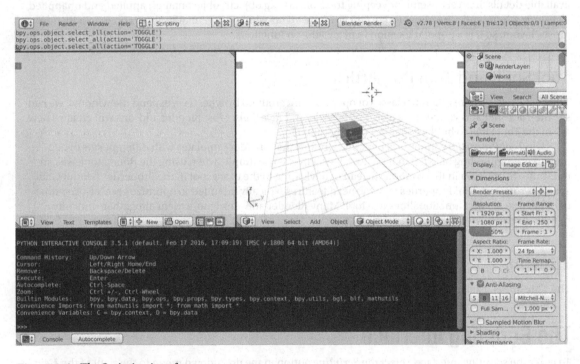

Figure 1-4. *The Scripting interface*

The Scripting layout, or some variant of it, will be where we do most of our work in Blender. We will discuss new components of the Blender interface introduced in Figure 1-5.

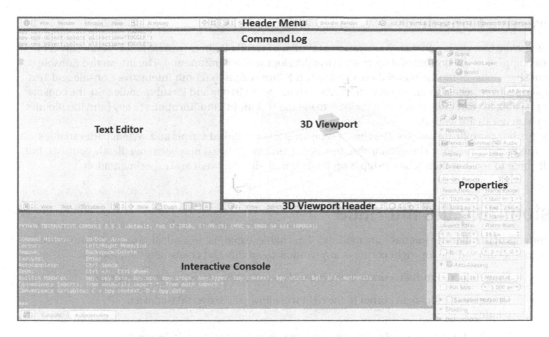

Figure 1-5. *Components of the Scripting interface*

Text Editor

We can edit Python scripts (and any other text files) in the *Text Editor*. We can click the *New* and *Open* buttons to create and open scripts, respectively. Once scripts are loaded, the menu bar at the bottom of the Text Editor will change to allow saving and switching between files.

Blender's Text Editor has some special properties pertaining to imports, system paths, and linked files in Python. We discuss this in detail later in this chapter and in future chapters when developing add-ons.

Command Log

The *Command Log* shows function calls made by the Blender interface during the session. This window is extremely useful when experimenting with scripts and learning about the API. If, for example, we translate the cube in the 3D Viewport using the red arrow, we get the output shown in Listing 1-1 in the Command Log.

Listing 1-1. Command Log Output from Translation Along x-Axis

```
bpy.ops.transform.translate(value=(3.05332, 0, 0), constraint_axis=(True, False, False),
                    constraint_orientation='GLOBAL', mirror=False, proportional='DISABLED',
                    proportional_edit_falloff='SMOOTH', proportional_size=1,
                    release_confirm=True)
```

The output in Listing 1-1 shows that we called the `translate()` function from the `transform` class of the `bpy.ops` submodule. The parameters are fairly verbose and often redundant in calls made from the interface, but they are straightforward enough that we can decipher what they mean and experiment with the function. We dig into code like this in the next chapter. While the act of *deciphering* is often the best and fastest way to learn about functions in Blender Python, we can also reference the official documentation for more detail. This is also discussed in the next chapter.

5

Interactive Console

The *Interactive Console* is a Python 3 environment similar to vanilla Python console and IPython consoles that often appear at the bottom of IDEs (interactive development environments). The Interactive Console does not share local or module-level data with the Text Editor scripts, but both Interactive Console and Text Editor scripts have access to the same global Blender data stored in bpy and its submodules. So, the console will not be able to read or modify variables local to the the scripts, but modifications to bpy (and the Blender session in general) are shared.

To further complicate matters, the console and scripts share linked scripts and system path variables during the Blender session. The relationship between these components may seem needlessly complex, but we will come to see that their relationship is optimal for both development and experimentation.

Customizing the Interface

Components of the Blender interface are modular, detachable, expandable, and all-around customizable. Users can drag around the top-right corner of any window to modify and create new windows.

- Dragging the top-right corner to the left will create a new window of the same type

- Dragging the top-right corner to the right will allow you to overtake adjacent windows

- Holding Shift and dragging the top-right corner in any direction will copy the component in a new detached window

Creating a 3D Viewport in a detachable window and duplicating the Text Editor is great way to use a dual-screen setup. Having two Text Editors available is very helpful for debugging custom modules. See Figure 1-6 for a screenshot of a dual-screen setup.

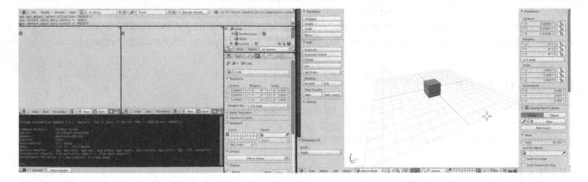

Figure 1-6. *Example of a dual-screen development interface*

Note that if your Tool Shelf or Tool Properties windows disappear when moving around the interface, press **T** on the keyboard while in the 3D Viewport to reveal them. Additionally, press **N** on the keyboard while in the 3D Viewport to reveal a new window, the *Object Properties*. This window is used very often in add-on development, specifically when we begin assigning custom Blender classes to our objects as parameters.

Starting Blender from the Command Line (for Debugging)

When developing Python scripts in Blender, it is very important that we start Blender from the command line. When we run scripts in Blender, if we get an error, the Command Log will show this message:

```
Python script fail, look in the console for now...
```

This message can be very confusing, because the Interactive Console will show nothing. What Blender means is: *Look in the terminal for now...* Unfortunately, most people do not open Blender via the terminal, and the error messages and tracebacks will go unnoticed unless we have a terminal running Blender in the background. Opening Blender via the terminal is the unofficial "Debug Mode" for Python developers. Blender has an official Debug Mode used by the core developers, but this is not generally helpful to us as API users.

To open Blender from the terminal, we must navigate to the Blender executable in a Blender distribution saved on our system. Make sure to have downloaded the Blender .zip or .bz2 file for the appropriate operating system from https://www.blender.org/download/. Save and unzip the folder in an easily accessible location. Windows users will open the command prompt, and UNIX users will open a terminal. Listings 1-2 and 1-3 show the commands required to open a Blender install sitting on the Desktop for Windows and UNIX users, respectively. Alternatively, Windows users can open Blender normally, then navigate to **Header Menu ➤ Window ➤ Toggle System Console** to view the terminal.

Listing 1-2. Opening Blender from the Command Line in Windows

```
# Assuming you are starting from C:\Users\%USERNAME%
cd Desktop\blender-2.78c-windows64
blender

# Navigating from anywhere on the Windows
# filesystem to Blender on the Desktop
cd C:\Users\%USERNAME%\Desktop\blender-2.78c-windows64
blender

# If an existing Blender install causes
# the wrong version to open, use blender.exe
cd C:\Users\%USERNAME%\Desktop\blender-2.78c-windows64
blender.exe
```

Listing 1-3. Opening Blender from the Command Line in UNIX

```
# Navigating to Blender on the Desktop from
# anywhere in the filesystem for Linux
cd ~/Desktop/blender-2.78c-linux-glibc211-x86_64
./blender

# Navigating to Blender in the home directory for OSX
cd ~/Desktop/blender-2.78c-OSX-10.6-x86_64
./blender
```

Now Blender is running from the terminal, and it will dump warnings and errors to the terminal. If we exit the terminal, Blender will also close. Developers should always open Blender from the command line to get detailed debugging information. We will generally keep the terminal minimized until we get an error, then maximize it to study the recent output.

Running Our First Python Script

With the information presented in this chapter, we can open a fresh Blender session with the command line, arrange the interface to a nice development layout, and be prepared to debug our Python code.

Our first objective will be to create a cube out of cubes. We will walk through the natural thought process of exploring Blender and the API to create a script that accomplishes our objective.

Finding the Function

First, we need to figure out which function adds a cube to the scene. Navigate to the 3D Viewport and go to **3D Viewport Header ➤ Add ➤ Meshes ➤ Cube**. Now navigate to the Command Log to verify that the function was executed as shown in Listing 1-4.

Listing 1-4. Command Log Output for Adding a Cube to the Scene

```
bpy.ops.mesh.primitive_cube_add(radius=1, view_align=False, enter_editmode=False,
                        location=(0, 0, 0), layers=(True, False, False, False, False,
                                                    False, False, False, False, False,
                                                    False, False, False, False, False,
                                                    False, False, False, False, False))
```

Testing the Function

Upon examination, we see many arguments that we do not need to accomplish our objective. We do not want to enter Edit Mode, we do not need to align the 3D Viewport to the object, and we are working in the first layer for now. We will guess that we do not need the arguments view_align, enter_editmode, and layers, and that their default values are acceptable. Additionally, we will assume that radius specifies the size of the cube, and location specifies the location. To test this, run Listing 1-5 in the Interactive Console.

Listing 1-5. Testing Defaults of primitive_cube_add()

```
# Make a bigger cube sitting in the first quadrant
bpy.ops.mesh.primitive_cube_add(radius=3, location=(5, 5, 5))
```

By running Listing 1-5 in the Interactive Console, we see no errors, and we see a large cube centered at (5, 5, 5) in the 3D Viewport. We can now confidently use the function in a script to accomplish our objective, making a cube of cubes.

Delete our big cube (and any other stray objects) from the scene in preparation to run our script. Use the **A** key in the 3D Viewport to toggle *Select All* and press the **X** key to be prompted to delete all selected objects.

Writing the Script

Make sure to go to **Text Editor ➤ New** to create a new script. To create a cube of cubes, we will nest three loops that iterate through our *x*, *y*, and *z* values. Copy Listing 1-6 into the Text Editor and go to **Text Editor ➤ Run Script.**

Listing 1-6. Creating a Cube of Cubes

```
import bpy

for k in range(5):
    for j in range(5):
        for i in range(5):
            bpy.ops.mesh.primitive_cube_add(radius=0.25, location=(i, j, k))
```

This script creates a cube 0.25 * 2 = 0.5 units wide, centered at every combination of whole number vertices such that $0 \leq x, y, z < 5$. The result is pictured in Figure 1-7.

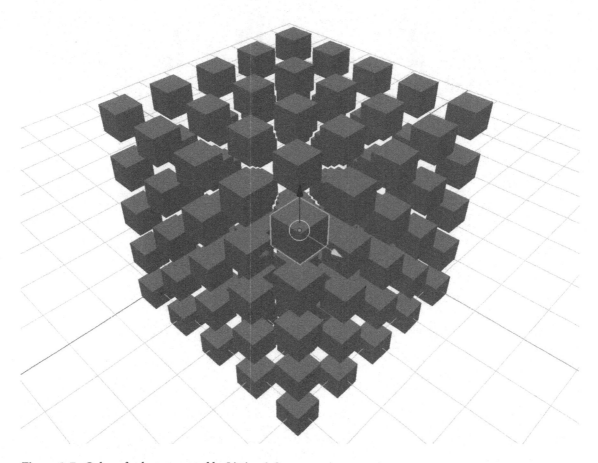

Figure 1-7. *Cubes of cubes generated by Listing 1-6*

■ **Note**   To find functions, classes, parameter lists, and minimal documentation, use the autocomplete feature of Blender's Interactive Console. With the mouse cursor in the window of the Interactive Console, begin typing a bpy function. Press **Ctrl+Space**, and Blender will show class and function information.

Conclusion

In the coming chapters, we expand on the process used to arrive at Listing 1-6, allowing us to create virtually anything in Blender. Using the vocabulary established in this chapter, we will be able to talk through advanced concepts in Blender Python scripting.

CHAPTER 2

The bpy Module

This chapter introduces and details major components of the bpy module. In doing so, we explain many important behaviors of Blender. We cover selection and activation, creation and deletion, scene management, and code abstraction.

The official documentation for the Blender Python API can be found by selecting a version of Blender at http://www.blender.org/api/. We are using Blender 2.78c in this text, so our documentation can be found at http://www.blender.org/api/blender_python_api_2_78c_release/.

Module Overview

We begin by giving some background on each submodule of bpy.

bpy.ops

As implied, this submodule contains operators. These are primarily functions for manipulating objects, similarly to the way Blender artists manipulate objects in the default interface. The submodule can also manipulate the 3D Viewport, renderings, text, and much more.

For manipulating 3D objects, the two most important classes are bpy.ops.object and bpy.ops.mesh. The object class contains functions for manipulating multiple selected objects at the same time as well as many general utilities. The mesh class contains functions for manipulating vertices, edges, and faces of objects one at a time, typically in Edit Mode.

There are currently 71 classes in the bpy.ops submodule, all fairly well-named and well-organized.

■ **Note**   Documentation for modules, submodules, and classes can be accessed directly by appending the Pythonic path to the object and .html to the home URL of your version's Blender documentation. For example, documentation for the bpy.ops.mesh class can be found here: www.blender.org/api/blender_python_api_2_78c_release/bpy.ops.mesh.html.

---

bpy.context

The bpy.context submodule is used to access objects and areas of Blender by various status criteria. The primary function of this submodule is to give Python developers a means of accessing the *current* data that a user is working with. If we create a button that permutes all of the selected objects, we can allow the user to select the objects of his choice, then permute all objects in bpy.context.select_objects.

© Chris Conlan 2017
C. Conlan, *The Blender Python API*, DOI 10.1007/978-1-4842-2802-9_2

We make frequent use of bpy.context.scene when building add-ons, as it is a required input to certain Blender objects. We can also use bpy.context to access the active objects, toggle between Object Mode and Edit Mode, and accept data from a grease pencil.

bpy.data

This submodule is used to access Blender's internal data. It can be difficult to interpret documentation on this specific module (the */bpy.data.html page points directly to a separate class), but we will rely heavily on it throughout this text. The bpy.data.objects class contains all of the data determining an object's shape and position. When we say the the previous submodule bpy.context is great for pointing us to groups of objects, we mean that bpy.context classes will generate references to datablocks of the bpy.data class.

bpy.app

This submodule is not entirely documented, but the information we are confident about thus far can be used to great effect in scripting and add-on development. The sub-submodule bpy.app.handlers is the only one we will concern ourselves with in this text. The handlers submodule contains special functions for triggering custom functions in response to events in Blender. Most commonly used is the frame change handle, which executes some function every time the 3D Viewport is updated (i.e., after a frame change).

bpy.types, bpy.utils, and bpy.props

These modules are discussed in detail in later chapters on add-on development. Readers may presently find the documentation in */bpy.types.html useful for describing classes of objects we are utilizing elsewhere.

bpy.path

This submodule is essentially the same as the os.path submodule that ships natively with Python. It is rarely useful to Blender Python developers outside of the core development team.

Selection, Activation, and Specification

The Blender interface was designed to be intuitive while also providing complex functionality. Certain operations logically apply to single objects where others can logically be used on one or many objects at the same time. To handle these scenarios, Blender developers created three ways to access an object and its data.

- *Selection*: One, many, or zero objects can be selected at once. Operations that use selected objects can perform that operation simultaneously on a single object or many objects.

- *Activation*: Only a single object can be active at any given time. Operations that work on the active object are typically more specific and drastic, thus cannot be intuitively performed on many things at once.

- *Specification*: (Python only) Python scripts can access objects by their names and write directly to their datablocks. While an operation that manipulates selected objects is typically a differential action like *translate, rotate,* or *scale,* writing data to specific objects is typically a declarative action like *position, orientation,* or *size.*

Selecting an Object

Before continuing, readers are encouraged to create a handful of different objects in the 3D Viewport to use as examples. Go to **3D Viewport Header ➤ Add** to see the object creation menu.

When we click around in the 3D Viewport with a right-click, objects highlight and unhighlight. When we hold the **Shift** key and click around, we are able to highlight multiple objects at once. These highlights in the 3D Viewport represent the selected objects. To list the selected objects, type the code in Listing 2-1 into the Interactive Console.

Listing 2-1. Getting a List of Selected Objects

```
# Outputs bpy.data.objects datablocks
bpy.context.selected_objects
```

As we alluded to earlier, the bpy.context submodule is great for fetching lists of objects based on their state within Blender. In this case, we fetched all the selected objects.

```
# Example output of Listing 2.1, list of bpy.data.objects datablocks
[bpy.data.objects['Sphere'], bpy.data.objects['Circle'], bpy.data.objects['Cube']]
```

In this case, a sphere named Sphere, a circle named Circle, and a cube named Cube were all selected in the 3D Viewport. We were returned a Python list of bpy.data.objects datablocks. Given the knowledge that all datablocks of this type have a name value, we can loop through the results of Listing 2-1 to access the names of the selected objects. See Listing 2-2, where we grab both the names and positions of the selected objects.

Listing 2-2. Getting a List of Selected Objects

```
# Return the names of selected objects
[k.name for k in bpy.context.selected_objects]

# Return the locations of selected objects
# (location of origin assuming no pending transformations)
[k.location for k in bpy.context.selected_objects]
```

Now that we know how to manually select objects, we need to automatically select objects based on some criteria. The requisite functions are in bpy.ops. Listing 2-3 creates a function that takes an object name as an argument and selects it, clearing all other selections by default. If the user specifies additive = True, the function will not clear other selections beforehand.

Listing 2-3. Programmatically Selecting Objects

```
import bpy

def mySelector(objName, additive=False):

    # By default, clear other selections
    if not additive:
      bpy.ops.object.select_all(action='DESELECT')

    # Set the 'select' property of the datablock to True
    bpy.data.objects[objName].select = True
```

13

```
# Select only 'Cube'
mySelector('Cube')

# Select 'Sphere', keeping other selections
mySelector('Sphere', additive=True)

# Translate selected objects 1 unit along the x-axis
bpy.ops.transform.translate(value=(1, 0, 0))
```

■ **Note**   To easily view the names of objects without Python scripting, navigate to the Properties window and select the orange cube icon. Now, active objects will show their name near the top of this subwindow, as is the case in Figure 2-1. Also, the bottom-left corner of the 3D Viewport will display the name of the active object. We discuss activation in the next subsection of this chapter.

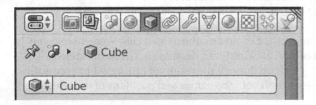

Figure 2-1. *Checking object names in the Blender interface*

Activating an Object

Activation, like selection, is an object state in Blender. Unlike selection, only one object can be active at any given time. This state is generally used for vertex, edge, and face manipulation of single objects. This state also has a close relationship with Edit Mode, which we discuss in detail later in this chapter.

When we left-click around the 3D Viewport, any object that we click will be highlighted. When we highlight a single object in this manner, Blender both selects and activates that object. If we hold **Shift** and **left-click** around the 3D Viewport, only the first object we click will be active.

Note the area of the Properties window pictured in Figure 2-1, where the name of the active object is displayed. Objects can also be activated via the menu at the bottom of Figure 2-1.

To access the active object in Python, type Listing 2-4 in the Interactive Console. Notice there are two equivalent bpy.context classes for accessing the active object. Just as with selected objects, we are returned a bpy.data.objects datablock, which we can operate on directly.

Listing 2-4. Accessing the Active Object

```
# Returns bpy.data.objects datablock
bpy.context.object

# Longer synonym for the above line
bpy.context.active_object

# Accessing the 'name' and 'location' values of the datablock
bpy.context.object.name
bpy.context.object.location
```

Listing 2-5 is an analogue to Listing 2-3 for activation. Since only one object can be active at any given time, the activation function is much simpler. We pass a `bpy.data.objects` datablock to a scene property that handles internal data on activation. Because Blender only allows a single object to be active, we can make a single assignment to `bpy.context.scene` and allow Blender's internal engine to sort out deactivation of other objects.

Listing 2-5. Programmatically Activating an Object

```
import bpy

def myActivator(objName):

    # Pass bpy.data.objects datablock to scene class
    bpy.context.scene.objects.active = bpy.data.objects[objName]

# Activate the object named 'Sphere'
myActivator('Sphere')

# Verify the 'Sphere' was activated
print("Active object:", bpy.context.object.name)

# Selected objects were unaffected
print("Selected objects:", bpy.context.selected_objects)
```

■ **Note**   When we introduce listings intended for use in the Text Editor rather than the Interactive Console (typically multi-line programs), we always import bpy. The bpy module is imported by default in the Interactive Console, but each run of a script in the Text Editor is an independent session that does not import bpy by default. Additionally, when we want to view output of a program in the Interactive Console, we will simply type the object we want to view information on. When we want to view output from the Text Editor, we use printing functions to send the output to the terminal with which Blender was opened. Otherwise, we would be unable to see output other than warnings and errors from the Text Editor scripts.

Specifying an Object (Accessing by Name)

This section details how to return `bpy.data.objects` datablocks by specifying the name of the object. Listing 2-6 shows how to access the `bpy.data.objects` datablock for an object given its name. Based on our discussion up to this point, Listing 2-6 may seem trivial. This circular nature of datablock referencing has a very important purpose.

Listing 2-6. Accessing an Object by Specification

```
# bpy.data.objects datablock for an object named 'Cube'
bpy.data.objects['Cube']

# bpy.data.objects datablock for an object named 'eyeballSphere'
bpy.data.objects['eyeballSphere']
```

Listing 2-7 is an analogue to Listings 2-3 and 2-5, but applies to *specification*. The goal of mySelector() and myActivator() were to return the datablock or datablocks of objects with a given state. In this case, mySpecifier() trivially returns the datablock.

Listing 2-7. Programmatically Accessing an Object by Specification

```
import bpy

def mySpecifier(objName):
    # Return the datablock
    return bpy.data.objects[objName]

# Store a reference to the datablock
myCube = mySpecifier('Cube')

# Output the location of the origin
print(myCube.location)

# Works exactly the same as above
myCube = bpy.data.objects['Cube']
print(myCube.location)
```

Pseudo-Circular Referencing and Abstraction

The bpy.data.objects datablocks have a very interesting property that highlights many of the wise architecting decisions made for the Blender Python API. With the goal of promoting modularity, extensibility, and liberal abstraction, bpy.data.objects datablocks were built to nest infinitely. We refer to this as *pseudo-circular referencing* because, while references are circular, they occur *within* rather than *between* objects, making the concept distinct from circular referencing.

See Listing 2-8 for trivial examples of datablocks making pseudo-circular references.

Listing 2-8. Pseudo-Circular Referencing

```
# Each line will return the same object type and memory address
bpy.data
bpy.data.objects.data
bpy.data.objects.data.objects.data
bpy.data.objects.data.objects.data.objects.data

# References to the same object can be made across datablock types
bpy.data.meshes.data
bpy.data.meshes.data.objects.data
bpy.data.meshes.data.objects.data.scenes.data.worlds.data.materials.data

# Different types of datablocks also nest
# Each of these lines returns the bpy.data.meshes datablock for 'Cube'
bpy.data.meshes['Cube']
bpy.data.objects['Cube'].data
bpy.data.objects['Cube'].data.vertices.data
bpy.data.objects['Cube'].data.vertices.data.edges.data.materials.data
```

Listing 2-8 showcases a powerful feature of the Blender Python API. When we append .data to an object, it returns a reference to the parent datablock. This behavior comes with some restrictions. For example, we cannot append .data.data to move from a bpy.data.meshes[] datablock to the bpy.data datablock. Nonetheless, this behavior will help us build clean and readable codebases that are naturally modular.

We will create tools in this text that enable us to build and manipulate objects in Blender without directly calling the bpy module. While pseudo-circular referencing seems trivial as we present it in Listing 2-8, readers will see that it often happens implicitly in toolkits when abstracting the bpy module.

Transformations with bpy

This section discusses major components of the bpy.ops.transorm class and its analogues elsewhere. It naturally expands on the theme of abstraction and introduces some helpful Blender Python tricks.

Listing 2-9 is a minimal set of tools for creating, selecting, and transforming objects. The bottom of the script runs some example transformations. Figure 2-2 shows the output from a test run of the minimal toolkit in the 3D Viewport.

Listing 2-9. Minimal Toolkit for Creation and Transformation (ut.py)

```python
import bpy

# Selecting objects by name
def select(objName):
    bpy.ops.object.select_all(action='DESELECT')
    bpy.data.objects[objName].select = True

# Activating objects by name
def activate(objName):
    bpy.context.scene.objects.active = bpy.data.objects[objName]

class sel:
    """Function Class for operating on SELECTED objects"""

    # Differential
    def translate(v):
        bpy.ops.transform.translate(
            value=v, constraint_axis=(True, True, True))

    # Differential
    def scale(v):
        bpy.ops.transform.resize(value=v, constraint_axis=(True, True, True))

    # Differential
    def rotate_x(v):
        bpy.ops.transform.rotate(value=v, axis=(1, 0, 0))

    # Differential
    def rotate_y(v):
        bpy.ops.transform.rotate(value=v, axis=(0, 1, 0))
```

```
    # Differential
    def rotate_z(v):
        bpy.ops.transform.rotate(value=v, axis=(0, 0, 1))

class act:
    """Function Class for operating on ACTIVE objects"""

    # Declarative
    def location(v):
        bpy.context.object.location = v

    # Declarative
    def scale(v):
        bpy.context.object.scale = v

    # Declarative
    def rotation(v):
        bpy.context.object.rotation_euler = v

    # Rename the active object
    def rename(objName):
        bpy.context.object.name = objName

class spec:
    """Function Class for operating on SPECIFIED objects"""

    # Declarative
    def scale(objName, v):
        bpy.data.objects[objName].scale = v

    # Declarative
    def location(objName, v):
        bpy.data.objects[objName].location = v

    # Declarative
    def rotation(objName, v):
        bpy.data.objects[objName].rotation_euler = v

class create:
    """Function Class for CREATING Objects"""

    def cube(objName):
        bpy.ops.mesh.primitive_cube_add(radius=0.5, location=(0, 0, 0))
        act.rename(objName)

    def sphere(objName):
        bpy.ops.mesh.primitive_uv_sphere_add(size=0.5, location=(0, 0, 0))
        act.rename(objName)

    def cone(objName):
        bpy.ops.mesh.primitive_cone_add(radius1=0.5, location=(0, 0, 0))
        act.rename(objName)
```

```python
# Delete an object by name
def delete(objName):

    select(objName)
    bpy.ops.object.delete(use_global=False)

# Delete all objects
def delete_all():

    if(len(bpy.data.objects) != 0):
        bpy.ops.object.select_all(action='SELECT')
        bpy.ops.object.delete(use_global=False)

if __name__ == "__main__":

    # Create a cube
    create.cube('PerfectCube')

    # Differential transformations combine
    sel.translate((0, 1, 2))

    sel.scale((1, 1, 2))
    sel.scale((0.5, 1, 1))

    sel.rotate_x(3.1415 / 8)
    sel.rotate_x(3.1415 / 7)

    sel.rotate_z(3.1415 / 3)

    # Create a cone
    create.cone('PointyCone')

    # Declarative transformations overwrite
    act.location((-2, -2, 0))
    spec.scale('PointyCone', (1.5, 2.5, 2))

    # Create a Sphere
    create.sphere('SmoothSphere')

    # Declarative transformations overwrite
    spec.location('SmoothSphere', (2, 0, 0))
    act.rotation((0, 0, 3.1415 / 3))
    act.scale((1, 3, 1))
```

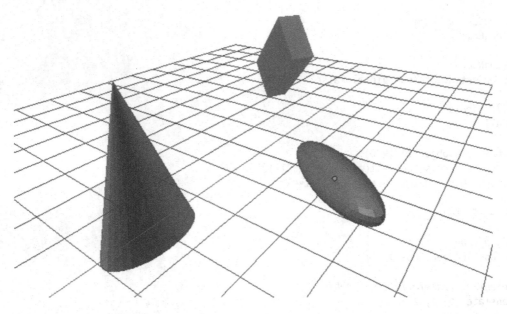

Figure 2-2. *Minimal toolkit test*

Notice the comment tags *differential* and *declarative*. There are a handful of ways to rotate, scale, and translate objects in Blender Python, but it is important to remember which functions dictate a form (declarative) and which functions modify a form (differential). Thankfully, the verbiage of the bpy functions and class values are fairly intuitive. For example, *rotate* is a verb, therefore differential, and *rotation* is a noun, therefore declarative.

Listing 2-9, which we will call ut.py, is a good starting point for a custom utility class.

In this book, we are interested in teaching the Blender Python API, not the author's ut.py module. While the ut.py module is a good reference and teaching tool, we will refrain from using its single-line function calls in future chapters. While those function calls may solve our problems in the short-term, they obscure class structures and parameters we would otherwise like to reinforce through repetition.

For now, we will do some cool visualizations with ut.py. In future chapters, we will add bulky and meaningful utility functions to it while treating the single-line functions as placeholders.

Visualizing Multivariate Data with the Minimal Toolkit

In this section, we visualize multivariate data with the toolkit in Listing 2-9. Before we begin, give this toolkit a Python filename of ut.py using the bar at the base of the Text Editor. Now, click the plus sign in the base of the Text Editor to create a new script. The file ut.py is now a linked script within the Blender Python environment, and we can import it into other scripts within the environment.

We will be visualizing the famous Fisher's Iris data set. This data set has five columns of data. The first four columns are numeric values describing dimensions of flower, and the final column is a categorical value describing the type of flower. There are three types of flowers in this data set: *setosa, versicolor*, and *virginica*.

Listing 2-10 serves as the header code for this example. It imports the necessary modules: our toolkit ut, the csv module, and urllib.request. We will fetch the data from a file repository with urllib, then parse it with csv. It is not necessary to understand all the code in Listing 2-10 to profit from this example.

Listing 2-10. Reading in iris.csv for the Exercise

```
import ut
import csv
import urllib.request

####################
# Reading in Data #
####################

# Read iris.csv from file repository
url_str = 'http://blender.chrisconlan.com/iris.csv'
iris_csv = urllib.request.urlopen(url_str)
iris_ob = csv.reader(iris_csv.read().decode('utf-8').splitlines())

# Store header as list, and data as list of lists
iris_header = []
iris_data = []

for v in iris_ob:
    if not iris_header:
        iris_header = v
    else:
        v = [float(v[0]),
             float(v[1]),
             float(v[2]),
             float(v[3]),
             str(v[4])]
        iris_data.append(v)
```

Visualizing Three Dimensions of Data

Since Blender is a 3D modeling suite, it seems most logical to visualize three dimensions of data. Listing 2-11 places a sphere at the (*x, y, z*) values of the 3D Viewport specified by the sepal length, sepal width, and petal length of each observation.

Listing 2-11. Visualizing Three Dimensions of Data

```
# Columns:
# 'Sepal.Length', 'Sepal.Width',
# 'Petal.Length', 'Petal.Width', 'Species'

# Visualize 3 dimensions
# Sepal.Length, Sepal.Width, and 'Petal.Length'

# Clear scene
ut.delete_all()

# Place data
for i in range(0, len(iris_data)):
    ut.create.sphere('row-' + str(i))
```

```
v = iris_data[i]
ut.act.scale((0.25, 0.25, 0.25))
ut.act.location((v[0], v[1], v[2]))
```

The resultant set of spheres appear in the 3D Viewport, as shown in Figure 2-3. Obviously, the 2D picture printed in this text does not do this model justice. Using Blender's mouse and keyboard movement tools, users can explore this data very intuitively.

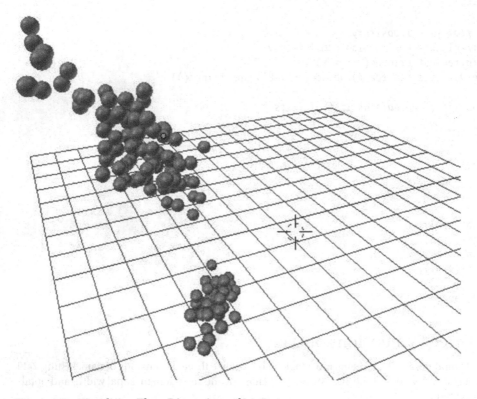

Figure 2-3. *Visualizing Three Dimensions of Iris Data*

Visualizing Four Dimensions of Data

Fortunately, there are more than three ways we can parameterize objects using Blender Python. To account for the final numeric variable, petal width, we will scale the spheres by the petal width. This will allow us to visualize and understand four dimensions of data within Blender. Listing 2-12 is a slight modification of the prior.

Listing 2-12. Visualizing Four Dimensions of Data

```
# Columns:
# 'Sepal.Length', 'Sepal.Width',
# 'Petal.Length', 'Petal.Width', 'Species'
```

```
# Visualize 4 dimensions
# Sepal.Length, Sepal.Width, 'Petal.Length',
# and scale the object by a factor of 'Petal.Width'

# Clear scene
ut.delete_all()

# Place data
for i in range(0, len(iris_data)):
    ut.create.sphere('row-' + str(i))
    v = iris_data[i]
    scale_factor = 0.2
    ut.act.scale((v[3] * scale_factor,) * 3)
    ut.act.location((v[0], v[1], v[2]))
```

The resultant set of spheres appear in the 3D Viewport, as shown in Figure 2-4. It is very apparent that the lower group of spheres has a very small sepal width. Figure 2-5 zooms in on this cluster of data.

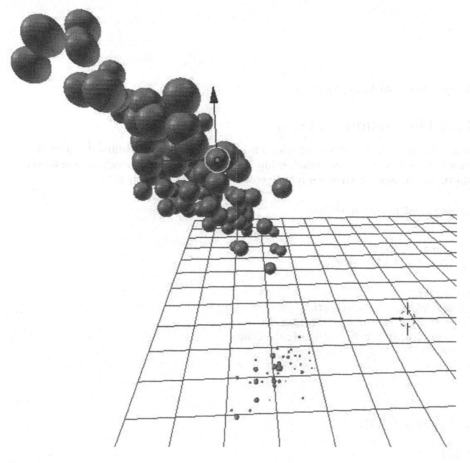

Figure 2-4. *Visualizing Four Dimensions of Iris Data*

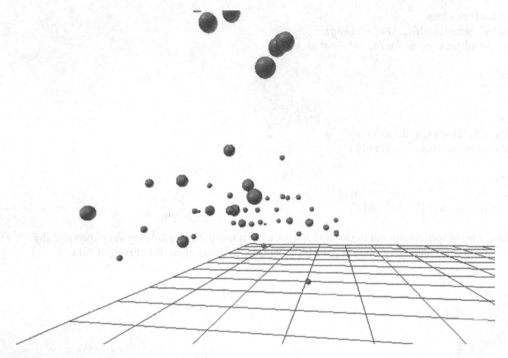

Figure 2-5. *Visualizing Four Dimensions of Iris Data Pt. 2*

Visualizing Five Dimensions of Data

From what we have seen up to this point, there exist at least two very distinct clusters within this data. We will dig into the flower species data to look for a relationship. To easily distinguish between types of flowers within the 3D Viewport, we can assign each flower type a geometric shape. See Listing 2-13.

Listing 2-13. Visualizing Five Dimensions of Data

```
# Columns:
# 'Sepal.Length', 'Sepal.Width',
# 'Petal.Length', 'Petal.Width', 'Species'

# Visualize 5 dimensions
# Sepal.Length, Sepal.Width, 'Petal.Length',
# and scale the object by a factor of 'Petal.Width'
# setosa = sphere, versicolor = cube, virginica = cone

# Clear scene
ut.delete_all()

# Place data
for i in range(0, len(iris_data)):

    v = iris_data[i]

    if v[4] == 'setosa':
        ut.create.sphere('setosa-' + str(i))
```

```
if v[4] == 'versicolor':
    ut.create.cube('versicolor-' + str(i))
if v[4] == 'virginica':
    ut.create.cone('virginica-' + str(i))

scale_factor = 0.2
ut.act.scale((v[3] * scale_factor,) * 3)
ut.act.location((v[0], v[1], v[2]))
```

The resultant output in the 3D Viewport (Figure 2-6) sheds light on the relationship between dimensions and species within the data. We see many cones, *virginica flowers*, at the peak of the larger cluster, and we see many cubes, *versicolor flowers*, at the bottom of that larger cluster. There is some overlap between the dimensions of these two species. The spheres, *setosa flowers*, make up the completely separated cluster of flowers with smaller dimensions.

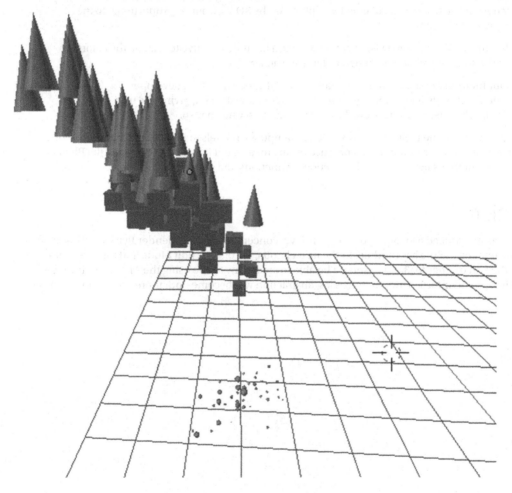

Figure 2-6. *Visualizing Five Dimensions of Iris Data*

Discussion

With fewer than 200 lines code, we have built a powerful proof-of-concept for an interactive multivariate data visualization software. Concepts like this can be extended with advanced API functions we have yet to cover, including texturing, GUI development, and vertex-level operations. At present, our example software can use improvement on the following fronts:

- No ability to scale data for the visualizer. The iris data worked nicely because the numeric values were conveniently in the range of (0, 0, 0) ± 10, which is about how many Blender units are easily viewable by default.

- We could investigate a better system for scaling objects such that they best represent the data. For example, the volume of a sphere is proportional to the cube of the radius, so we may consider passing the cubic root of the data value as radius to the `scale()` function. The argument can be made that this creates a more intuitive visualization. The same argument can be made for taking the square root of the data value, because the area covered by a sphere in the 3D Viewport is proportional to the square of its radius.

- In our five-dimensional visualization, it would be more intuitive to change the colors of the spheres rather than assign a shape to each species.

- Our method of reading in data is static and GUI-less. An add-on developer would naturally like to apply this methodology to any data set, giving the user comprehensive controls over what he views and how he does so.

Note that, via `ut.py`, the main script was able to manipulate models in Blender without calling or importing bpy. This is not a recommended practice by any means, but it is exemplar of how the Blender Python environment treats bpy as a global collection of functions and data.

Conclusion

This chapter has introduced a lot of important high-level concepts about the Blender Python API, as well as detailed core functions of the bpy module. In the next chapter, we discuss Edit Mode and the `bmesh` module in detail. By the end of Chapter 3, users should be able to create any shape using the API. As we introduce more complicated and interdependent processes, abstraction will become both more important and more laborious.

CHAPTER 3

■ ■ ■

The bmesh Module

So far, we have talked about ways to create, manage, and transform whole objects. Blender's default *mode* is Object Mode, which allows us to select and manipulate one or many objects, typically with transformations that can be appropriately applied to groups of disparate objects, such as rotation and translation.

Blender begins to shine as a 3D art suite when we enter Edit Mode. This mode allows us to select one or many vertices of a single object to perform advanced and detailed transformations. As one would expect, most operations that are intended for Edit Mode cannot be performed in Object Mode and vice versa.

The bmesh module deals almost exclusively in Edit Mode operations. Thus, we will give a proper treatment of the differences between Object Mode and Edit Mode before diving into the functionalities of bmesh.

Edit Mode

To manually enter Edit Mode as a traditional Blender 3D artist would, go to **3D Viewport Header ➤ Interaction Mode Menu ➤ Edit Mode**, as pictured in Figure 3-1. Use the same menu for switching back into Object Mode.

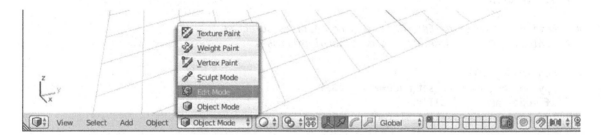

Figure 3-1. *Toggling Between Edit and Object Mode*

When switching into Edit Mode, the activated object at that time will be the only object the user can edit for that session of Edit Mode. If the user want to manipulate a different object in Edit Mode, he must switch back to Object Mode to activate the desired object first. Only then, after switching back into Edit Mode with the desired object activated, will he be able to manipulate it. Refer to the section "Selection, Activation, and Specification" in Chapter 2 if the verbiage regarding selection and activation is unclear at this point. Remember that we can always run bpy.context.object in the Interactive Console to check the name of the activated object.

To programmatically switch between Object Mode and Edit Mode, use the two commands in Listing 3-1.

C. Conlan, *The Blender Python API*, DOI 10.1007/978-1-4842-2802-9_3

Listing 3-1. Switching Between Object and Edit Mode

```
# Set mode to Edit Mode
bpy.ops.object.mode_set(mode="EDIT")

# Set mode to Object Mode
bpy.ops.object.mode_set(mode="OBJECT")
```

Selecting Vertices, Edges, and Planes

To begin manipulating details of single objects, we must be able to select specific parts. We will wrap our mode-setting functions in our ut.py module, then discuss how bmesh is used to select specific parts of an object. In doing so, we will work through a few quirks and version compatibility pitfalls of bmesh and the vertex indexing protocol in Blender.

Switching Between Edit and Object Modes Consistently

Listing 3-2 implements a wrapper function for switching between Object Mode and Edit Mode. We will insert this in the ut.py toolkit we began building in Chapter 2. The only modification we have made to the vanilla bpy.ops method is to deselect all vertices, edges, and planes of the active object when we enter Edit Mode. Currently, Blender's protocol for determining which parts of the object are selected upon entry in Edit Mode is opaque and unwieldy. We will take the safest and most consistent approach by deselecting every part of the object whenever we enter Edit Mode.

When we enter Object Mode from Edit Mode, Blender simply restores the active and selected objects from when we first entered Edit Mode. This behavior is reliable and understandable, so we will not modify the standard behavior of bpy.ops.object.mode_set(mode = "OBJECT").

Listing 3-2. Wrapper Function for Switching Between Object and Edit Mode

```
# Place in ut.py

# Function for entering Edit Mode with no vertices selected,
# or entering Object Mode with no additional processes

def mode(mode_name):
    bpy.ops.object.mode_set(mode=mode_name)
    if mode_name == "EDIT":
        bpy.ops.mesh.select_all(action="DESELECT")
```

■ **Note**   If you're editing a custom module like ut.py multiple times in the same Blender session, make sure to call importlib.reload(ut) on the module to see import the un-cached version into Blender. See Listing 3-3 for an example.

Listing 3-3. Editing Custom Modules, Live Within a Blender Session

```
# Will use the cached version of ut.py from
# your first import of the Blender session
import ut
ut.create.cube('myCube')
```

```
# Will reload the module from the live script of ut.py
# and create a new cached version for the session
import importlib
importlib.reload(ut)
ut.create.cube('myCube')

# This is what the header of your main script
# should look like when editing custom modules
import ut
import importlib
importlib.reload(ut)

# Code using ut.py ...
```

Instantiating a bmesh Object

In Blender, bmesh objects are fairly heavy-handed and computationally expensive when compared to other core data structures. To maintain efficiency, Blender gives much of the data and instance management work to the user to manage via the API. We will continue to see examples of this as we explore the bmesh module. See Listing 3-4 for an example of instantiating a bmesh object. In general, instantiating a bmesh object requires us to pass a bpy.data.meshes datablock to bmesh.from_edit_mesh() while in Edit Mode.

Listing 3-4. Instantiating a bmesh Object

```
import bpy
import bmesh

# Must start in object mode
# Script will fail if scene is empty
bpy.ops.object.mode_set(mode='OBJECT')
bpy.ops.object.select_all(action='SELECT')
bpy.ops.object.delete()

# Create a cube and enter Edit Mode
bpy.ops.mesh.primitive_cube_add(radius=1, location=(0, 0, 0))
bpy.ops.object.mode_set(mode='EDIT')

# Store a reference to the mesh datablock
mesh_datablock = bpy.context.object.data

# Create the bmesh object (named bm) to operate on
bm = bmesh.from_edit_mesh(mesh_datablock)

# Print the bmesh object
print(bm)
```

If we try running these commands in the Interactive Console, we may get a different result. Instances of bmesh objects are not persistent. Unless Blender detects that it is being actively used, the bmesh object will dereference the mesh datablock, garbage collect internal data, and return <BMesh dead at some_memory_ address>. This is a desirable behavior given the space and compute power required to maintain a bmesh object, but it does require programmers to execute extra commands to keep it alive. We will encounter these commands as we build functions for selecting specific parts of 3D objects.

Selecting Parts of a 3D Object

To select parts of a bmesh object, we manipulate the select Booleans of each BMesh.verts, BMesh.edges, and BMesh.faces object. Listing 3-5 gives an example of selecting parts of a cube.

Notice the numerous calls to ensure_lookup_table() in Listing 3-5. We use these functions to remind Blender to keep certain parts of the BMesh object from being garbage-collected between operations. These functions take up minimal processing power, so we can call them liberally without much consequence. It is better to over-call them than to under-call them, because debugging this error:

ReferenceError: BMesh data of type BMesh has been removed

Can be nightmarish in large codebases with no protocol for ensure_lookup_table().

Listing 3-5. Selecting Parts of 3D Objects

```
import bpy
import bmesh

# Must start in object mode
bpy.ops.object.mode_set(mode='OBJECT')
bpy.ops.object.select_all(action='SELECT')
bpy.ops.object.delete()

# Create a cube and enter Edit Mode
bpy.ops.mesh.primitive_cube_add(radius=1, location=(0, 0, 0))
bpy.ops.object.mode_set(mode='EDIT')

# Set to "Face Mode" for easier visualization
bpy.ops.mesh.select_mode(type = "FACE")

# Register bmesh object and select various parts
bm = bmesh.from_edit_mesh(bpy.context.object.data)

# Deselect all verts, edges, faces
bpy.ops.mesh.select_all(action="DESELECT")

# Select a face
bm.faces.ensure_lookup_table()
bm.faces[0].select = True

# Select an edge
bm.edges.ensure_lookup_table()
bm.edges[7].select = True

# Select a vertex
bm.verts.ensure_lookup_table()
bm.verts[5].select = True
```

Readers will notice that we run bpy.ops.mesh.select_mode(type = "FACE"). This concept has not been covered up to this point but is important to understand to properly use advanced Edit Mode functions. Typically, Blender artists click one of the three options in 3D Viewport Header, as shown in Figure 3-2. The buttons in Figure 3-2 correspond to the VERT, EDGE, and FACE arguments in bpy.ops.mesh.select_mode(). Right now, this will only affect how we visualize selections in Edit Mode. We select FACE for this example because it is the best mode for visualizing all three types simultaneously. Later in the chapter, we will discuss some functions in Edit Mode whose behavior will change depending on this selection.

Figure 3-2. *Toggling various selection modes*

Edit Mode Transformations

This section discusses simple transformations like translation and rotation in Edit Mode, as well as advanced transformations like randomization, extrusion, and subdivision.

Basic Transformations

Conveniently enough, we can use the same functions we used for Object Mode transformations in Chapter 2 to operate on individual parts of a 3D object. We will give some examples Listing 3-6 using the bpy.ops submodule introduced in Listing 2-9. See Figure 3-3 for output of slightly deformed cubes.

Listing 3-6. Basic Transformations in Edit Mode

```
import bpy
import bmesh

# Must start in object mode
bpy.ops.object.mode_set(mode='OBJECT')
bpy.ops.object.select_all(action='SELECT')
bpy.ops.object.delete()

# Create a cube and rotate a face around the y-axis
bpy.ops.mesh.primitive_cube_add(radius=0.5, location=(-3, 0, 0))
bpy.ops.object.mode_set(mode='EDIT')
bpy.ops.mesh.select_all(action="DESELECT")

# Set to face mode for transformations
bpy.ops.mesh.select_mode(type = "FACE")

bm = bmesh.from_edit_mesh(bpy.context.object.data)
bm.faces.ensure_lookup_table()
bm.faces[1].select = True
bpy.ops.transform.rotate(value = 0.3, axis = (0, 1, 0))

bpy.ops.object.mode_set(mode='OBJECT')
```

```
# Create a cube and pull an edge along the y-axis
bpy.ops.mesh.primitive_cube_add(radius=0.5, location=(0, 0, 0))
bpy.ops.object.mode_set(mode='EDIT')
bpy.ops.mesh.select_all(action="DESELECT")

bm = bmesh.from_edit_mesh(bpy.context.object.data)
bm.edges.ensure_lookup_table()
bm.edges[4].select = True
bpy.ops.transform.translate(value = (0, 0.5, 0))

bpy.ops.object.mode_set(mode='OBJECT')

# Create a cube and pull a vertex 1 unit
# along the y and z axes
# Create a cube and pull an edge along the y-axis
bpy.ops.mesh.primitive_cube_add(radius=0.5, location=(3, 0, 0))
bpy.ops.object.mode_set(mode='EDIT')
bpy.ops.mesh.select_all(action="DESELECT")

bm = bmesh.from_edit_mesh(bpy.context.object.data)
bm.verts.ensure_lookup_table()
bm.verts[3].select = True
bpy.ops.transform.translate(value = (0, 1, 1))

bpy.ops.object.mode_set(mode='OBJECT')
```

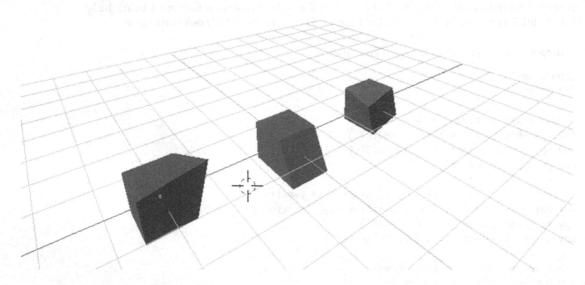

Figure 3-3. *Deforming cubes with edit mode operations*

Advanced Transformations

We could not hope to cover all of the tools included in Blender for editing meshes, so we will cover a handful in this section and flush out more using examples at the end of the chapter. Listing 3-7 implements the extrude, subdivide, and randomize operators. See Figure 3-4 for the intended output.

Listing 3-7. Extrude, Subdivide, and Randomize Operators

```
import bpy
import bmesh

# Will fail if scene is empty
bpy.ops.object.mode_set(mode='OBJECT')
bpy.ops.object.select_all(action='SELECT')
bpy.ops.object.delete()

# Create a cube and extrude the top face away from it
bpy.ops.mesh.primitive_cube_add(radius=0.5, location=(-3, 0, 0))
bpy.ops.object.mode_set(mode='EDIT')
bpy.ops.mesh.select_all(action="DESELECT")

# Set to face mode for transformations
bpy.ops.mesh.select_mode(type = "FACE")

bm = bmesh.from_edit_mesh(bpy.context.object.data)
bm.faces.ensure_lookup_table()
bm.faces[5].select = True
bpy.ops.mesh.extrude_region_move(TRANSFORM_OT_translate =
        {"value": (0.3, 0.3, 0.3),
         "constraint_axis": (True, True, True),
         "constraint_orientation" :'NORMAL'})

bpy.ops.object.mode_set(mode='OBJECT')

# Create a cube and subdivide the top face
bpy.ops.mesh.primitive_cube_add(radius=0.5, location=(0, 0, 0))
bpy.ops.object.mode_set(mode='EDIT')
bpy.ops.mesh.select_all(action="DESELECT")

bm = bmesh.from_edit_mesh(bpy.context.object.data)
bm.faces.ensure_lookup_table()
bm.faces[5].select = True
bpy.ops.mesh.subdivide(number_cuts = 1)

bpy.ops.mesh.select_all(action="DESELECT")
bm.faces.ensure_lookup_table()
bm.faces[5].select = True
bm.faces[7].select = True
bpy.ops.transform.translate(value = (0, 0, 0.5))

bpy.ops.object.mode_set(mode='OBJECT')

# Create a cube and add a random offset to each vertex
bpy.ops.mesh.primitive_cube_add(radius=0.5, location=(3, 0, 0))
bpy.ops.object.mode_set(mode='EDIT')
bpy.ops.mesh.select_all(action="SELECT")
bpy.ops.transform.vertex_random(offset = 0.5)

bpy.ops.object.mode_set(mode='OBJECT')
```

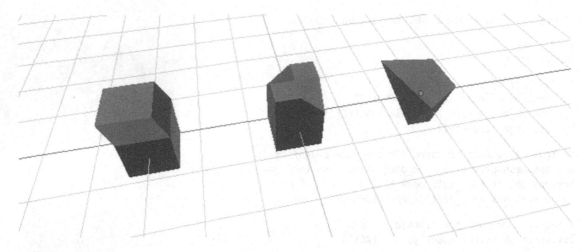

Figure 3-4. Extrude, Subdivide, and Randomize Operators

Note on Indexing and Cross-Compatibility

Readers may have noticed that the indices of vertices, edges, and faces in 3D objects are arranged in no particular order. In the example scripts thus far, the author had manually located the indices in advance rather than discover them programmatically. For example, when manipulating the tops of cubes in Listing 3-7, the author determined in advance that ut.act.select_face(bm, 5) would select the face on the top side of the cube. This was determined through trial-and-error testing.

Using trial-and-error tests to discover the index number of a part of an object is an acceptable practice in general, but suffers from a number of disadvantages. Within any given version of Blender, indexing semantics should be considered replicable but untamable.

- Default indices of objects vary wildly across different versions of Blender. The author has noted major compatibility issues in add-ons relying on hardcoded indices across different versions of Blender. Major differences were noted between version 2.77 and version 2.78 in add-ons relying on hardcoded indices.

- Behavior of indexing after certain transformations is very unwieldy. See Figure 3-5 for an example of the vertex indices of a default plane, a plane after three insets, and a plain after two subdivisions. The indices in these planes conform to no particular logical pattern. Variance among transformations is another source of cross-version incompatibility.

- Add-ons using hardcoded indices are very limited in user-interaction possibilities. An add-on that uses hardcoded indices can run successively, but can very rarely if ever engage in back-and-forth interaction with the user.

The workaround to this issue is *selection by characteristic*. To select a vertex by a characteristic, we loop through each vertex in the object and run bm.verts[i].select = True on vertices that meet a criteria. The same holds for edges and faces. On paper, this method looks very computationally expensive and algorithmically complex, but you will find it is surprisingly fast and modular. Plugins that use pure selection by characteristic can often run successfully on many versions of Blender simultaneously. Unfortunately, implementing this opens up a conceptual can of worms in Blender regarding local and global coordinate systems. We flush this out as well in the next section.

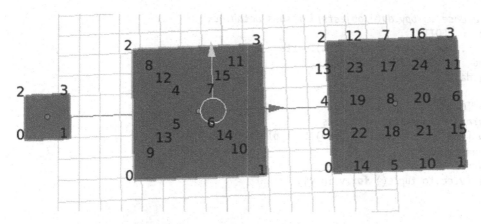

Figure 3-5. *Default, inset, and subdivided planes with vertex indices labeled*

Global and Local Coordinates

Blender stores many sets of coordinate data for each part of each object. In most cases, we will only be concerned with two sets of coordinates: *global coordinates* **G** and *local coordinates* **L**. When we perform transformations on objects, Blender stores these transformations as part of a transformation matrix, **T**. Blender will, at some point, apply the transformation matrix to the local coordinates. After Blender applies the transformation matrix, the local coordinates will be equal to the global coordinates, and the transformation matrix will be the identity matrix.

Within the 3D Viewport, we view global coordinates **G** = **T** * **L** always.

We can control when Blender applies transformations with bpy.ops.object.transform_apply(). This will not change the appearance of the objects, rather it will set **L** equal to **G** and set **T** equal to the identity.

We can use this to our advantage to easily select specific parts of objects. If we delay execution of bpy. ops.object.transform_apply() by not running it and not exiting Edit Mode, we can maintain two data sets **G** and **L**. In practice, **G** is very useful for positioning objects relative to others, and **L** is very easy to loop through to fetch indices.

See Listing 3-8 for functions to access global and local coordinates of an object. Given the bpy.data. meshes[].vertices datablock as v, v.co gives the local coordinates and bpy.data.objects[].matrix_ world * v.co gives the global coordinates. Thankfully, this datablock can be accessed in both Object Mode and Edit Mode. We will build mode-independent functions for accessing these coordinates. See Listing 3-8 for functions that fetch each set of coordinates independent of the mode.

These functions sacrifice some clarity in exchange for brevity and efficiency. In this code, v is a list of tuples that represents our matrix **L**, and obj.matrix_world is a Python matrix that represents our transformation matrix **T**.

Listing 3-8. Fetching Global and Local Coordinates

```
def coords(objName, space='GLOBAL'):

    # Store reference to the bpy.data.objects datablock
    obj = bpy.data.objects[objName]
```

```
    # Store reference to bpy.data.objects[].meshes datablock
    if obj.mode == 'EDIT':
        v = bmesh.from_edit_mesh(obj.data).verts
    elif obj.mode == 'OBJECT':
        v = obj.data.vertices

    if space == 'GLOBAL':
        # Return T * L as list of tuples
        return [(obj.matrix_world * v.co).to_tuple() for v in v]
    elif space == 'LOCAL':
        # Return L as list of tuples
        return [v.co.to_tuple() for v in v]

class sel:

    # Add this to the ut.sel class, for use in object mode
    def transform_apply():
        bpy.ops.object.transform_apply(
            location=True, rotation=True, scale=True)
```

See Listing 3-9 for an example of the behavior of local and global coordinates. We print the first two coordinate triples of a cube before transformation, immediately after transformation, and after transform_apply(). This makes sense on paper and in the code editor. Running Listing 3-9 in the Interactive Console line-by-line highlights the interesting behavior of transform_apply(). After translating the cube, readers will see the cube move, but the local coordinates will remain the same. After running transform_apply(), the cube will not move, but the local coordinates will update to match the global coordinates.

Listing 3-9. Behavior of Global and Local Coordinates and Transform Apply

```
import ut
import importlib
importlib.reload(ut)

import bpy

# Will fail if scene is empty
bpy.ops.object.mode_set(mode='OBJECT')
bpy.ops.object.select_all(action='SELECT')
bpy.ops.object.delete()

bpy.ops.mesh.primitive_cube_add(radius=0.5, location=(0, 0, 0))
bpy.context.object.name = 'Cube-1'

# Check global and local coordinates
print('\nBefore transform:')
print('Global:', ut.coords('Cube-1', 'GLOBAL')[0:2])
print('Local: ', ut.coords('Cube-1', 'LOCAL')[0:2])

# Translate it along x = y = z
# See the cube move in the 3D viewport
bpy.ops.transform.translate(value = (3, 3, 3))
```

```
# Check global and local coordinates
print('\nAfter transform, unapplied:')
print('Global: ', ut.coords('Cube-1', 'GLOBAL')[0:2])
print('Local: ', ut.coords('Cube-1', 'LOCAL')[0:2])

# Apply transformation
# Nothing changes in 3D viewport
ut.sel.transform_apply()

# Check global and local coordinates
print('\nAfter transform, applied:')
print('Global: ', ut.coords('Cube-1', 'GLOBAL')[0:2])
print('Local: ', ut.coords('Cube-1', 'LOCAL')[0:2])


############################ Output ##########################
# Before transform:
# Global: [(-0.5, -0.5, -0.5), (-0.5, -0.5, 0.5)]
# Local: [(-0.5, -0.5, -0.5), (-0.5, -0.5, 0.5)]
#
# After transform, unapplied:
# Global: [(2.5, 2.5, 2.5), (2.5, 2.5, 3.5)]
# Local: [(-0.5, -0.5, -0.5), (-0.5, -0.5, 0.5)]
#
# After transform, applied:
# Global: [(2.5, 2.5, 2.5), (2.5, 2.5, 3.5)]
# Local: [(2.5, 2.5, 2.5), (2.5, 2.5, 3.5)]
##############################################################
```

In the next section, we use this concept to combat the issue presented in Figure 3-5 and unlock the full power of Edit Mode in Blender.

Selecting Vertices, Edges, and Faces by Location

See Listing 3-10 for two functions that work together to facilitate selection of vertices, edges, and faces per their location in global and local coordinate systems. The function we specify as ut.act.select_by_loc() looks and is very complex, but does not use any Blender concepts that we have not introduced up to this point. The author believes this function should be included as part of the bmesh module because it is so widely applicable.

Listing 3-10. Function for Selecting Pieces of Objects by Location

```
# Add in body of script, outside any class declarations
def in_bbox(lbound, ubound, v, buffer=0.0001):
    return lbound[0] - buffer <= v[0] <= ubound[0] + buffer and \
        lbound[1] - buffer <= v[1] <= ubound[1] + buffer and \
        lbound[2] - buffer <= v[2] <= ubound[2] + buffer

class act:

    # Add to ut.act class
    def select_by_loc(lbound=(0, 0, 0), ubound=(0, 0, 0),
                    select_mode='VERT', coords='GLOBAL'):
```

```
# Set selection mode, VERT, EDGE, or FACE
selection_mode(select_mode)

# Grab the transformation matrix
world = bpy.context.object.matrix_world

# Instantiate a bmesh object and ensure lookup table
# Running bm.faces.ensure_lookup_table() works for all parts
bm = bmesh.from_edit_mesh(bpy.context.object.data)
bm.faces.ensure_lookup_table()

# Initialize list of vertices and list of parts to be selected
verts = []
to_select = []

# For VERT, EDGE, or FACE ...
# 1. Grab list of global or local coordinates
# 2. Test if the piece is entirely within the rectangular
#    prism defined by lbound and ubound
# 3. Select each piece that returned True and deselect
#    each piece that returned False in Step 2

if select_mode == 'VERT':
    if coords == 'GLOBAL':
        [verts.append((world * v.co).to_tuple()) for v in bm.verts]
    elif coords == 'LOCAL':
        [verts.append(v.co.to_tuple()) for v in bm.verts]

    [to_select.append(in_bbox(lbound, ubound, v)) for v in verts]
    for vertObj, select in zip(bm.verts, to_select):
        vertObj.select = select

if select_mode == 'EDGE':
    if coords == 'GLOBAL':
        [verts.append([(world * v.co).to_tuple()
                       for v in e.verts]) for e in bm.edges]
    elif coords == 'LOCAL':
        [verts.append([v.co.to_tuple() for v in e.verts])
         for e in bm.edges]

    [to_select.append(all(in_bbox(lbound, ubound, v)
                      for v in e)) for e in verts]
    for edgeObj, select in zip(bm.edges, to_select):
        edgeObj.select = select

if select_mode == 'FACE':
    if coords == 'GLOBAL':
        [verts.append([(world * v.co).to_tuple()
                       for v in f.verts]) for f in bm.faces]
    elif coords == 'LOCAL':
        [verts.append([v.co.to_tuple() for v in f.verts])
         for f in bm.faces]
```

```
        [to_select.append(all(in_bbox(lbound, ubound, v)
                              for v in f)) for f in verts]
    for faceObj, select in zip(bm.faces, to_select):
        faceObj.select = select
```

Listing 3-11 gives an example of using ut.act.select_by_loc() to select pieces of a sphere and transform them. Remember that the first two arguments to this function are the lowest corner and highest corner of a rectangular prism in the 3D. If the entire piece (vertex, edge, face) falls within the rectangular prism, it will be selected.

Listing 3-11. Selecting and Transforming Pieces of a Sphere

```
import ut
import importlib
importlib.reload(ut)

import bpy

# Will fail if scene is empty
bpy.ops.object.mode_set(mode='OBJECT')
bpy.ops.object.select_all(action='SELECT')
bpy.ops.object.delete()

bpy.ops.mesh.primitive_uv_sphere_add(size=0.5, location=(0, 0, 0))
bpy.ops.transform.resize(value = (5, 5, 5))
bpy.ops.object.mode_set(mode='EDIT')
bpy.ops.mesh.select_all(action='DESELECT')

# Selects upper right quadrant of sphere
ut.act.select_by_loc((0, 0, 0), (1, 1, 1), 'VERT', 'LOCAL')

# Selects nothing
ut.act.select_by_loc((0, 0, 0), (1, 1, 1), 'VERT', 'GLOBAL')

# Selects upper right quadrant of sphere
ut.act.select_by_loc((0, 0, 0), (5, 5, 5), 'VERT', 'LOCAL')

# Mess with it
bpy.ops.transform.translate(value = (1, 1,1))
bpy.ops.transform.resize(value = (2, 2, 2))

# Selects lower half of sphere
ut.act.select_by_loc((-5, -5, -5), (5, 5, -0.5), 'EDGE', 'GLOBAL')

# Mess with it
bpy.ops.transform.translate(value = (0, 0, 3))
bpy.ops.transform.resize(value = (0.1, 0.1, 0.1))

bpy.ops.object.mode_set(mode='OBJECT')
```

Checkpoint and Examples

Up to this point we have made a lot of additions to ut.py. For an up-to-date version with all of the additions we have made thus far in the book, visit blender.chrisconlan.com/ut_ch03.py.

Given this version of ut.py, we will try some fun examples. See Listing 3-12 for a random shape growth algorithm. A brief algorithm randomly (and sloppily) selects a chunk of space in which the object resides, then extrudes the selected portion along the vertical normal of the selected surface. To extrude along the vertical normal of a surface, we simply run ut.act.extrude((0, 0, 1)), since this function uses the local orientation of the surface by default.

The algorithm lets us build both elegant and wacky shapes. The type of result is mostly dependent on which shape we supply in the ut.create call near the top of the script. See Figures 3-6 and 3-7 for examples of Listing 3-12 with a cube and sphere, respectively.

Listing 3-12. Random Shape Growth

```
import ut
import importlib
importlib.reload(ut)

import bpy

from random import randint
from math import floor

# Must start in object mode
bpy.ops.object.select_all(action='SELECT')
bpy.ops.object.delete()

# Create a cube
bpy.ops.mesh.primitive_cube_add(radius=0.5, location=(0, 0, 0))
bpy.context.object.name = 'Cube-1'

bpy.ops.object.mode_set(mode='EDIT')
bpy.ops.mesh.select_all(action="DESELECT")

for i in range(0, 100):

    # Grab the local coordinates
    coords = ut.coords('Cube-1', 'LOCAL')

    # Find the bounding box for the object
    lower_bbox = [floor(min([v[i] for v in coords])) for i in [0, 1, 2]]
    upper_bbox = [floor(max([v[i] for v in coords])) for i in [0, 1, 2]]

    # Select a random face 2x2x1 units wide, snapped to integer coordinates
    lower_sel = [randint(l, u) for l, u in zip(lower_bbox, upper_bbox)]
    upper_sel = [l + 2 for l in lower_sel]
    upper_sel[randint(0, 2)] -= 1

    ut.act.select_by_loc(lower_sel, upper_sel, 'FACE', 'LOCAL')

    # Extrude the surface along it aggregate vertical normal
    bpy.ops.mesh.extrude_region_move(TRANSFORM_OT_translate =
            {"value": (0, 0, 1),
             "constraint_axis": (True, True, True),
             "constraint_orientation" :'NORMAL'})
```

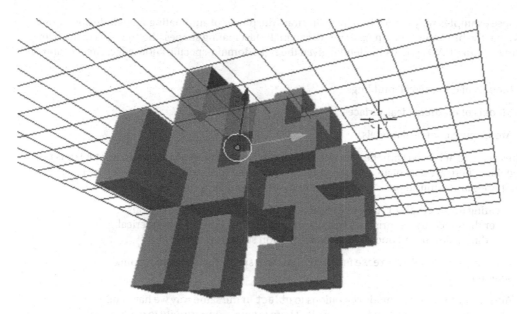

Figure 3-6. *Random cube extrusion with 500 iterations*

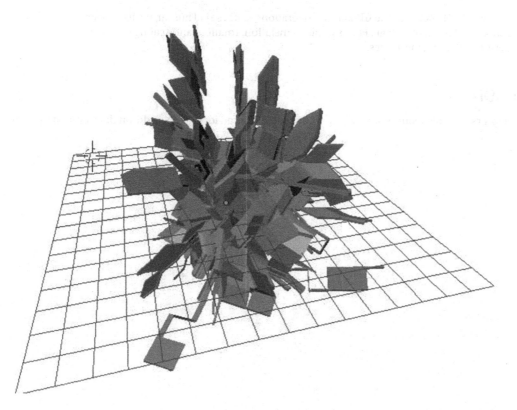

Figure 3-7. *Random sphere extrusion with 1000 iterations*

While these examples may seem trivial, they illustrate the power of automating Edit Mode operations in Blender. While the brief algorithm in Listing 3-12 can make fascinating shapes, the concepts within can be used to create entire CAD systems in Blender given the right domain-specific knowledge. Great examples include:

- Models of commercial buildings

- Models of mathematical surfaces

- Atomic and chemical models

All of these can be achieved with the concepts discussed in this chapter. As it stands, our toolkit is not very case-specific. There are a lot of areas where it can be improved to accommodate modeling needs of different disciplines and applications. Notable ways to customize and improve our toolkit include:

- Creating ut.act.select_by_loc() functions that support selection regions other than rectangular prisms. There is potential use for cylindrical, spherical, two-dimensional, and one-dimensional selection surfaces.

- Creating additional ut.create functions and case-specific automated naming schema for them.

- Adding additional edit mode operations to ut.act in the same way we have added ut.act.extrude and ut.act.subdivide. There is ample opportunity to explore and further parameterize these functions.

- Adding LOCAL, NORMAL, and GIMBAL axis operations to ut.sel. Thus far, we have been using the default of GLOBAL. For example, translation, rotation, and scaling can all be performed along these axes.

Conclusion

In the next chapters, we talk about basic rendering concepts required for effective add-on development in Blender.

CHAPTER 4

■ ■ ■

Topics in Modeling and Rendering

This chapter introduces and details particular topics in 3D modeling and rendering. While very general, these topics become important in Chapter 5 and the remainder of the text as we build more advanced tools and plugins. Readers are introduced to many utilities and pitfalls commonly known to 3D artists, game developers, and rendering software engineers. Equipped with this knowledge, readers will be able to better serve the needs of these professionals in script and add-on development.

Specifying a 3D Model

3D models are complex digital assets that can be made up of many different components. Where we typically think of the *mesh* as the most important structure that constitutes the shape of the asset, meshes are made of *faces*, which consist of *vertices* arranged by *indices*. The mesh can contain *normal vectors* or *normals*, which can be specified with the vertices or faces, depending on the file format. When we refer to these terms in the abstract, we are discussing 3D modeling topics generally, not as they are specifically defined in Blender.

We begin our discussion of 3D models with purely the meshes, consisting of vertices, indices, faces, and normals. From there, we discuss more advanced and specific features of 3D models as an extension of our discussion of meshes.

Specifying Meshes

For the purpose of this chapter, we consider that a basic mesh is defined by its faces and normal vectors. See the following definitions of the aforementioned components:

- *Vertices* are real-valued triplets specifying a location in 3D space, typically represented as (x, y, z). For reasons we discuss, it is common to see the same point specified multiple times throughout a file specifying a 3D mesh. In 3D modeling, the z-axis or the y-axis is most often used to represent the vertical axis. In Blender, the z-axis is the vertical axis. We will use this format throughout the text.

- *Indices* are positive integer-valued triplets that specify faces using a series of vertices, typically represented as (i, j, k). Given a list of N vertices indexed as $1, ..., N$, a face in 3D space can be specified by a triplet of any three unique integers in $1, ..., N$. This concept extends itself very logically to allow us to define meshes by reusing pre-specified vertices. For reasons we explain, the order of the integers is important in determining the direction in which the face is visible. The concept of indexing reused tuple values is often extended to other tuples such as normals and UVs in practice.

© Chris Conlan 2017
C. Conlan, *The Blender Python API*, DOI 10.1007/978-1-4842-2802-9_4

- *Faces* are determined by integer triplets of indices referencing some three vertices. From our definitions, we naturally arrive at the fact that a three-vertex face in 3D space requires a total of nine real-valued data points. It is important to note that faces in 3D space are only visible in a single direction. Given a rotating camera and a single face in 3D space, the user will only be able to view the face from a single direction. From the other direction, the face will appear totally transparent. This is a native and expected behavior of many 3D renderers that we will learn to control for. Note that Blender does not exhibit this single-direction behavior by default, but Blender will not automatically control or correct for it when exporting to other file formats.

- *Normal Vectors* are real-valued triplets that define how the mesh interacts with lights and cameras in a scene. At the moment, we are concerned only with normals as they are directly assigned to points rather than normal maps that 3D artists may already by familiar with. As the name implies, the camera and lighting in a scene interacts with the mesh under the assumption that the normal vectors *lie normal* to the faces it is illuminating. This is not always a trivial question, as we will see with our cube examples. Normal vectors also affect the direction in which a face is viewable and the direction in which it is transparent, as referenced in the definition of faces.

Specifying Textures

The purpose of textures in 3D models is to map a 2D image onto a 3D surface, typically using an existing 2D art asset. The coordinate convention we use for this is the (u, v) coordinate system. In other areas of mathematics, when discussing 2D projections of 3D surfaces, we typically use the (u, v) coordinate system to clearly denote that we are working in a space separate from the (x, y, z) coordinate system.

Texture coordinates are very intuitive. If we would like to stretch an image over a rectangular surface, we specify the list of *uv* coordinates $[(0.0, 0.0), (1.0, 0.0), (0.0, 1.0), (1.0, 1.0)]$ to stretch the full image, face-up, left-to-right, over the surface we are looking at. This is assuming that coordinates 1 through 4 in our model represent the bottom-left, bottom-right, top-left, and top-right coordinates of the surface from our perspective. See Figure 4-1 for an example of this vanilla texturing scheme.

Figure 4-1. Vanilla texturing scheme on a cube

If we want to stretch, shrink, or duplicate the image across the surface, we simply adjust the *uv* coordinates by the appropriate factors. For example, the tile the image three times across the surface of the cube, we enter *uv* coordinates $[(0.0, 0.0), (3.0, 0.0), (0.0, 3.0), (3.0, 3.0)]$. See Figure 4-2 for an example of a tiled texture.

Figure 4-2. *Repeated texturing scheme on a cube*

We will not work with textures through Blender's Python API until Chapter 8, but the concept of *uv* coordinates for textures is important to understand as we discuss 3D models and file formats.

Common File Formats

We begin by listing common file formats and explaining their respective advantages and uses. We use these formats in conjunction with our definitions of 3D objects in the beginning of the chapter to further illustrate these concepts.

Wavefront (.obj and .mtl)

The Wavefront geometric (.obj) and materials (.mtl) specification formats work in conjunction to specify meshes and textures. They are written in such a way that the .obj file can stand on its own to specify solely geometry. The .obj file is very minimal and easy to understand, making it ideal for use as a standard notation for discussing the shapes of 3D objects.

See Listing 4-1 for an example of simple square in the *xy*-plane with the .obj format. We will refrain from explaining the .mtl file in detail, as it is less pertinent to our discussion of rendering concepts.

Listing 4-1. Simple Square in the .obj Format

```
# Use hashes to leave comments in .obj files
# The 'o' tag is used to name objects
# all data following an 'o' tag is considered
# to have this name until another name is entered
o MySimpleFace

# Vertices are entered with the 'v' tag as
# space-delimited (x, y, z) tuples
v -1.00 0.00 1.00
v 1.00 0.00 1.00
v -1.00 0.00 -1.00
v 1.00 0.00 -1.00
```

```
# Texture coordinate are entered with the 'vt' tag as
# space-delimited (u, v) tuples, between 0 and 1
vt 0.00 1.00
vt 1.00 1.00
vt 0.00 0.00
vt 1.00 0.00

# Normal vectors are entered with the 'vn' tag as
# space-delimited (x, y, z) tuples, can be normal vectors if desired
vn 0.0000 1.0000 0.0000

# Indices are entered with the 'f' (for face) tag as
# space-delimited triplets of v, vt, and vn indices as
# f v_i/vt_i/vn_i v_j/vt_j/vn_j v_k/vt_k/vn_k
# Faces can have any number (three or more) coplanar points
f 2/2/1 3/3/1 1/1/1
f 2/2/1 4/4/1 3/3/1

# Alternatively, the faces section for this face can be
# written as a single coplanar quadrilateral:
f 1/1/1 2/2/1 4/4/1 3/3/1

# Alternatively, the texture coordinates can be
# excluded with double slashes
f 1//1 2//1 4//1 3//1
```

We see in Listing 4-1 a specification in the .obj file format for a simple face with the following characteristics:

- Two units long by two units wide

- Centered at the origin, normal vector facing upward along the z-axis

- Some texture oriented along the positive x and y axes

We will see in the following examples that the .obj format is fairly mature and flexible in comparison to others.

STL (STereoLithography)

The STL file format is commonly used by engineers and CAD software. It is verbose when compared to the .obj format, but comes with a binary specification to compensate for its inefficiency. Most STL exporters (including Blender's) use the binary specification by default, making the files illegible for humans without the aid of special software. We only work with the text format of the file in this text.

See Listing 4-2 for our simple face as in Listing 4-1 specified in the STL format. STL supports normal vectors and faces, but does not use indices or support texture coordinates. As can be seen in Listing 4-2, we must specify the same normal vector twice and a total of six vertices to specify a quadrilateral face in STL. In addition, STL does not support specification of more than three coplanar points. Curiously, where most 3D file formats allow normal vectors to be assigned to points, STL only allows normal vectors to be assigned on the face level.

The structure is fairly self-explanatory. Every facet normal x y z initializes a face, then each outer loop-endloop pair holds the ordered vertices of the face. Each vertex is specified as vertex x y z within the loop.

Listing 4-2. Simple Face in the STL Format (Text Form)

```
solid MyFace
    facet normal     0.0     0.0     1.0
        outer  loop
            vertex    -1.0    -1.0    0.0
            vertex     1.0    -1.0    0.0
            vertex    -1.0     1.0    0.0
        endloop
    endfacet
    facet normal     0.0     0.0     1.0
        outer  loop
            vertex     1.0    -1.0    0.0
            vertex     1.0     1.0    0.0
            vertex    -1.0     1.0    0.0
        endloop
    endfacet
endsolid MyFace
```

PLY (Polygon File Format)

This file format was built by Stanford to work with 3D scanning software. It has close roots in the C language and many open source tools for working directly with it. Our discussion of 3D mesh formats should start to feel repetitive. The PLY format is essentially a stripped-down version of .obj with additional metadata that only supports vertices and faces, not normal vectors or textures.

Some metadata in the header is fairly standard, including the ply, format, and property tags. We will not delve into the property tags. Just know that they refer to C-level data types for cooperation with existing C libraries. The element vertex and element face lines specify how many lines of the file refer to vertices and faces, respectively. In our example, we have element vertex 4 and element face 1 because we are specifying a face. It is worth noting the PLY format supports specification of more than three coplanar points.

See Listing 4-3 for an example of a face.

Listing 4-3. Simple Face in the PLY Format

```
ply
format ascii 1.0
comment specifies a simple face
element vertex 4
property float32 x
property float32 y
property float32 z
element face 1
property list uint8 int32 vertex_indices
end_header
-1 -1 0
1 -1 0
1 1 0
-1 1 0
4 1 0 3 2
```

Blender (.blend) Files and Interchange Formats

Especially in light of the preceding examples, Blender's native file format and in-memory data structures are very complex. Blender supports operations on vertices, edges, and faces with noncoplanar vertices. All the while, Blender manages complex data related to textures, sounds, animations, rigs, lights, and more. These .blend files are represented in binary and not intended to be human-readable. Thankfully, we can continue to access and manipulate Blender's internal data safely through the Python API.

The difference in complexity and completeness between .blend files and the aforementioned .obj, .stl, and .ply files is intentional. While all of these files represent 3D models in one way or another, .blend files are not designed to be exported and imported in other 3D modeling suites. The file formats discussed above are called *interchange* formats, meaning they intentionally represent a common and well-defined subset of features that can be ported easily between modeling software and renderers.

While developers have made attempts in the past to create complete interoperability between specific 3D modeling suite like 3DS Max, AutoCAD, and Maya, and Blender, they necessarily fall short of capturing all of the features any one suite supports. Thus, we settle on interchange formats to keep communications and expectations consistent.

Minimal Specification of Basic Objects

It is important to discuss some of the theory behind specification of 3D models so that we can assess the efficiency and capabilities of various 3D file formats. We will reference the file formats discussed in the previous section to help illustrate.

Definition of a Cube

A cube is a three-dimensional object with six faces consisting of squares of equal lengths. A cube contains 6 faces, 12 edges, and 8 vertices. The square faces of a cube can be treated as compositions of two right triangles with leg lengths equal to the square length. Note that any object in 3D space can be defined by float and integer values, where floats specify locations and directions in 3D space and integers specify related indices. 3D objects also require normal vectors, which can be assigned to vertices or faces.

We will use this information to construct tables detailing the data density of different 3D specification schema.

Naive Specification

To naively specify a 3D cube, we will specify each of the $6 * 2 = 12$ required triangular faces independently of one another as well as assign an independent normal vector to each point. This should result in $12 * 3 = 36$ vertices and $12 * 3 = 36$ normal vectors. We can write this in .obj format, as in Listing 4-4. Figure 4-3 shows a visualization of the data structure of this model.

The naivety of this model is defined by:

- Needless repetition of vertex coordinates

- Needless repetition of normal vector directions

- Needless use of vertex normals in place of face normals

Listing 4-4. Naively Defined Cube

```
o NaiveCube

# (36 * 3) + (36 * 3) = 216 floats
# (12 * 3) + (12 * 3) = 72 integers

v 1.000000 -1.000000 -1.000000
v 1.000000 -1.000000 1.000000
v -1.000000 -1.000000 1.000000
v -1.000000 -1.000000 -1.000000
v 1.000000 1.000000 -0.999999
v 0.999999 1.000000 1.000001
v -1.000000 1.000000 1.000000
v -1.000000 1.000000 -1.000000
v 1.000000 -1.000000 -1.000000
v 1.000000 -1.000000 -1.000000
v 1.000000 -1.000000 1.000000
v 1.000000 -1.000000 1.000000
v -1.000000 -1.000000 -1.000000
v -1.000000 -1.000000 -1.000000
v 1.000000 1.000000 -0.999999
v 1.000000 1.000000 -0.999999
v -1.000000 -1.000000 1.000000
v -1.000000 -1.000000 1.000000
v 0.999999 1.000000 1.000001
v 0.999999 1.000000 1.000001
v -1.000000 1.000000 1.000000
v -1.000000 1.000000 1.000000
v -1.000000 1.000000 -1.000000
v -1.000000 1.000000 -1.000000
v 1.000000 -1.000000 -1.000000
v -1.000000 -1.000000 1.000000
v 0.999999 1.000000 1.000001
v -1.000000 1.000000 -1.000000
v 1.000000 -1.000000 -1.000000
v 1.000000 -1.000000 1.000000
v 1.000000 1.000000 -0.999999
v -1.000000 -1.000000 1.000000
v -1.000000 -1.000000 1.000000
v 0.999999 1.000000 1.000001
v -1.000000 1.000000 -1.000000
v -1.000000 1.000000 -1.000000

vn 0.0000 -1.0000 0.0000
vn 0.0000 1.0000 0.0000
vn 1.0000 -0.0000 0.0000
vn 0.0000 -0.0000 1.0000
vn -1.0000 -0.0000 -0.0000
vn 0.0000 0.0000 -1.0000
vn 0.0000 -1.0000 0.0000
vn 0.0000 1.0000 0.0000
```

```
vn 1.0000 -0.0000 0.0000
vn 0.0000 -0.0000 1.0000
vn -1.0000 -0.0000 -0.0000
vn 0.0000 0.0000 -1.0000
vn 0.0000 -1.0000 0.0000
vn 0.0000 1.0000 0.0000
vn 1.0000 -0.0000 0.0000
vn 0.0000 -0.0000 1.0000
vn -1.0000 -0.0000 -0.0000
vn 0.0000 0.0000 -1.0000
vn 0.0000 -1.0000 0.0000
vn 0.0000 1.0000 0.0000
vn 1.0000 -0.0000 0.0000
vn 0.0000 -0.0000 1.0000
vn -1.0000 -0.0000 -0.0000
vn 0.0000 0.0000 -1.0000
vn 0.0000 -1.0000 0.0000
vn 0.0000 1.0000 0.0000
vn 1.0000 -0.0000 0.0000
vn 0.0000 -0.0000 1.0000
vn -1.0000 -0.0000 -0.0000
vn 0.0000 0.0000 -1.0000
vn 0.0000 -1.0000 0.0000
vn 0.0000 1.0000 0.0000
vn 1.0000 -0.0000 0.0000
vn 0.0000 -0.0000 1.0000
vn -1.0000 -0.0000 -0.0000
vn 0.0000 0.0000 -1.0000

f 9//1 17//13 13//25
f 24//2 20//14 16//26
f 15//3 12//15 10//27
f 6//4 18//16 2//28
f 3//5 23//17 14//29
f 1//6 8//18 5//30
f 29//7 11//19 32//31
f 36//8 22//20 34//32
f 31//9 19//21 30//33
f 27//10 21//22 33//34
f 26//11 7//23 35//35
f 25//12 4//24 28//36
```

In other words, naive 3D specifications do not reuse vertices or normals through indexing by treating every face as a wholly independent triangle. In addition, using vertex normals rather than face normals in simple cases such as a cube can increase waste. This model would benefit greatly from:

- Removing repeated vertices
- Specifying triangular faces as square faces
- Removing repeated normals and/or using face normals
- Properly utilizing indices to organize vertices and normals

It is worth noting that this format has the same level of complexity as the `.stl` format barring STL's use of face normals.

We will show next how non-repeating vertices and normals can shrink the model size without increasing complexity.

Using Indices to Share Vertices and Normals

Listing 4-5 shows a `.obj` file with shared vertices and normals. When the file is able to properly use indices and not duplicate float data, we only need a total of 42 floats. In the next example, we will take advantage of coplanar surfaces to reduce the total number of integers. Visually, this data looks the same as in Figure 4-3, we have only reduced repetition in the float data.

Listing 4-5. Cube with Shared Vertices and Normals

```
o SharingCube

# (8 * 3) + (6 * 3) = 42 floats
# (12 * 3) + (12 * 3) = 72 integers

v 1.000000 -1.000000 -1.000000
v 1.000000 -1.000000 1.000000
v -1.000000 -1.000000 1.000000
v -1.000000 -1.000000 -1.000000
v 1.000000 1.000000 -0.999999
v 0.999999 1.000000 1.000001
v -1.000000 1.000000 1.000000
v -1.000000 1.000000 -1.000000

vn 0.0000 -1.0000 0.0000
vn 0.0000 1.0000 0.0000
vn 1.0000 -0.0000 0.0000
vn 0.0000 -0.0000 1.0000
vn -1.0000 -0.0000 -0.0000
vn 0.0000 0.0000 -1.0000

f 1//1 3//1 4//1
f 8//2 6//2 5//2
f 5//3 2//3 1//3
f 6//4 3//4 2//4
f 3//5 8//5 4//5
f 1//6 8//6 5//6
f 1//1 2//1 3//1
f 8//2 7//2 6//2
f 5//3 6//3 2//3
f 6//4 7//4 3//4
f 3//5 7//5 8//5
f 1//6 4//6 8//6
```

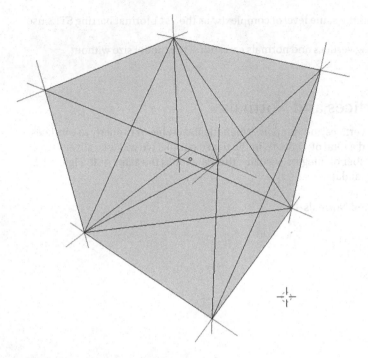

Figure 4-3. *Data structure of naively specified cube*

Using Coplanar Vertices to Reduce Face Count

Listing 4-6 shows a .obj file where each face of the cube is specified in whole. Because we know the faces of the cube are all collections of coplanar points, we can specify them as a single face. While renderers will still interpret the cube as a collection of triangular faces, the .obj file format allows us to specify N-dimensional surfaces with coplanar vertices. Figure 4-4 shows a visual representation of this data structure.

Listing 4-6. Cube with Coplanar Surfaces as Single Faces

```
o CoplanarFaceCube

# (8 * 3) + (6 * 3) = 42 floats
# (6 * 4) + (6 * 4) = 48 integers

v -1.000000 -1.000000 1.000000
v -1.000000 1.000000 1.000000
v -1.000000 -1.000000 -1.000000
v -1.000000 1.000000 -1.000000
v 1.000000 -1.000000 1.000000
v 1.000000 1.000000 1.000000
v 1.000000 -1.000000 -1.000000
v 1.000000 1.000000 -1.000000
```

```
vn -1.0000 0.0000 0.0000
vn 0.0000 0.0000 -1.0000
vn 1.0000 0.0000 0.0000
vn 0.0000 0.0000 1.0000
vn 0.0000 -1.0000 0.0000
vn  0.0000 1.0000 0.0000

f 1//1 2//1 4//1 3//1
f 3//2 4//2 8//2 7//2
f 7//3 8//3 6//3 5//3
f 5//4 6//4 2//4 1//4
f 3//5 7//5 5//5 1//5
f 8//6 4//6 2//6 6//6
```

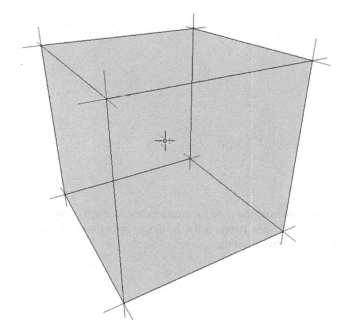

Figure 4-4. *Face-planar, vertex-sharing, normal-sharing cube*

There is not much repetition to be observed here. The last repetitive characteristic is specification of the normal vector index at each point of each face. We present a theoretical `.obj` file next that uses face vertices.

Using Face Vertices to Simplify Indices

Listing 4-7 shows a theoretical `.obj` file where each face of the cube is assigned to the same normal. Because cubes have well-defined face normals, it is easy for us to specify them within a data structure. Normally in `.obj` files, we would repetitively specify the indices of vertex normals. The rendering process would then compute a composition of the vertex normals to determine how to shade the concerned face. In this theoretical `.obj` file, we will specify the vertex indices at the face level rather than the point level. The file is called "theoretical" because `.obj` files do not actually support face normals, although other common file formats do. We will continue to use the `.obj` format in this example for sake of consistency, but note that this file with not import. See Figure 4-5 for a visual representation of this data structure.

53

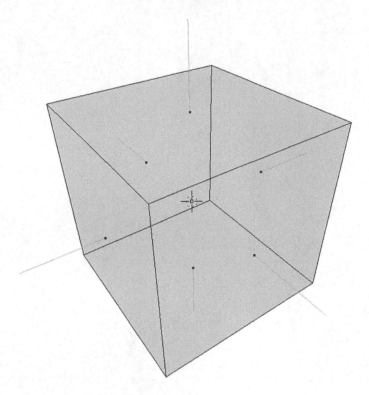

Figure 4-5. *Cube with face normals*

The next iteration will reduce the complexity by binarizing the cube into the renderer itself. This is a special case only applicable to very common and simple shapes. Rarely will a developer have the ability to customize this functionality in the renderer itself, but it is worth noting.

Listing 4-7. Cube with Face Normals

```
o FaceNormalsCube

# Theoretical .obj format, not valid
# (8 * 3) + (6 * 3) = 42 floats
# (6 * 4) + (6 * 1) = 30 integers

v -1.000000 -1.000000 1.000000
v -1.000000 1.000000 1.000000
v -1.000000 -1.000000 -1.000000
v -1.000000 1.000000 -1.000000
v 1.000000 -1.000000 1.000000
v 1.000000 1.000000 1.000000
v 1.000000 -1.000000 -1.000000
v 1.000000 1.000000 -1.000000
```

```
vn -1.0000 0.0000 0.0000
vn 0.0000 0.0000 -1.0000
vn 1.0000 0.0000 0.0000
vn 0.0000 0.0000 1.0000
vn 0.0000 -1.0000 0.0000
vn 0.0000 1.0000 0.0000

# Face and normals defined as:
# f (v_1, v_2, v_3, v_4)//n_1
f (1 2 4 3)//1
f (3 4 8 7)//2
f (7 8 6 5)//3
f (5 6 2 1)//4
f (3 7 5 1)//5
f (8 4 2 6)//6
```

Representing a Cube as a Primitive

Primitives loosely refer to very common objects that are pre-built into a 3D software package. Most notably for this discussion, primitives in renderers are binarized versions of common objects that will always outperform the equivalent text file specification (.obj, .stl, etc.) in load time. When possible, look into your renderer's documentation to find opportunities to add simple objects, typically cubes, spheres, cylinders, cones, and tori, using the renderer's default primitives. This is not to say that the in-memory specifications of the objects are more spatially efficient than any others, but only that they have the advantage of already being binarized.

Summary

We discussed four sequentially more efficient methods of specifying a cube, ending with the final option of using primitives. See the following table for a summary of the results. We have determined the size of the .obj file through command-line tools. We have estimated the in-memory size of the object using the fact that, in 32-bit systems, floats and integers in C++ are four bytes. The percentage change in in-memory size is substantial enough at every step to justify making any of these efficiency adjustments.

Method	No. Floats	No. Integers	.obj Size (KB)	In-Memory Size (KB)	In-Mem %Δ
Naive	216	72	2.28	1.15	0%
Add Triplet Sharing	42	72	0.61	0.46	60%
Use Coplanar Surfaces	42	48	0.54	0.36	22%
Use Face Normals	42	30	0.50	0.29	20%

The in-memory percentage change for triplet sharing is a compelling reason to always favor .obj and .ply over .stl whenever possible. Familiarity with information discussed in this section is critical for Blender Python API developers. While Blender is very powerful, it gives us the opportunity to be both wasteful and efficient.

Common Errors in Procedural Generation

We use the language established in this chapter to illustrate some common problems with procedurally generated models and what steps to take to debug them.

Concentric Normals

When generating models and exporting to various interchange and rendering formats, it is very easy for normal vectors to be ignored or misassigned. Blender handles much of the normal vector management process for us in the 3D Viewport, so these issues are rarely uncovered pre-export. One very common bug we encounter is unexplainable wonky lighting. The issue typically comes down to normal management and can be solved with a few function calls or button clicks in Blender itself.

See Listing 4-8 for an example of a cube's .obj file, which has been improperly given concentric normals. See Listing 4-9 for an example of a cube correctly exported with planar normals. These cubes were each rendered in WebGL to show how the normals affect lighting when exported to other renderers. See Figures 4-6 and 4-7 for the renderings of the concentric and planar cube models.

The concentric cube is lit and shaded as though it were a sphere, whereas the planar cube is lit and shaded logically, treating the top side as a sort of tabletop. Looking through Listing 4-8, we see that each vertex in the cube is matched to a normal vector that is equal to the vertex scaled by $1/\sqrt{3} \approx 0.5773$. This is a dangerous behavior in some exporters where, if explicit normal information is not found, it will default to creating unit vectors out of scaled vertices. This prevents the exporter from failing, but results in a poorly lit and often unrecognizable object.

This problem is common to hard-surface modelers that typically work with large planar surfaces. To organic modelers that create high-poly models, this problem can more easily go undiagnosed.

Listing 4-8. Cube with Concentric Normals

```
o ConcentricCube
v 1.000000 -1.000000 -1.000000
v 1.000000 -1.000000 1.000000
v -1.000000 -1.000000 1.000000
v -1.000000 -1.000000 -1.000000
v 1.000000 1.000000 -0.999999
v 0.999999 1.000000 1.000001
v -1.000000 1.000000 1.000000
v -1.000000 1.000000 -1.000000

vn 0.5773503 -0.5773503 -0.5773503
vn 0.5773503 -0.5773503 0.5773503
vn -0.5773503 -0.5773503 0.5773503
vn -0.5773503 -0.5773503 -0.5773503
vn 0.5773503 0.5773503 -0.5773497
vn 0.5773497 0.5773503 0.5773508
vn -0.5773503 0.5773503 0.5773503
vn -0.5773503 0.5773503 -0.5773503

f 1//1 3//3 4//4
f 8//8 6//6 5//5
f 5//5 2//2 1//1
f 6//6 3//3 2//2
f 3//3 8//8 4//4
```

```
f 1//1 8//8 5//5
f 1//1 2//2 3//3
f 8//8 7//7 6//6
f 5//5 6//6 2//2
f 6//6 7//7 3//3
f 3//3 7//7 8//8
f 1//1 4//4 8//8
```

Listing 4-9. Cube with Planar Normals

```
o PlanarCube
v 1.000000 -1.000000 -1.000000
v 1.000000 -1.000000 1.000000
v -1.000000 -1.000000 1.000000
v -1.000000 -1.000000 -1.000000
v 1.000000 1.000000 -0.999999
v 0.999999 1.000000 1.000001
v -1.000000 1.000000 1.000000
v -1.000000 1.000000 -1.000000

vn 0.0000 -1.0000 0.0000
vn 0.0000 1.0000 0.0000
vn 1.0000 0.0000 0.0000
vn -0.0000 -0.0000 1.0000
vn -1.0000 -0.0000 -0.0000
vn 0.0000 0.0000 -1.0000

f 1//1 2//1 3//1 4//1
f 5//2 8//2 7//2 6//2
f 1//3 5//3 6//3 2//3
f 2//4 6//4 7//4 3//4
f 3//5 7//5 8//5 4//5
f 5//6 1//6 4//6 8//6
```

Figure 4-6. *Concentric normals (smooth shading) in WebGL*

■ **Note**   Blender's built-in exporters (including `.obj` and `.stl`) will rarely, if ever, exhibit this behavior under normal circumstances. This behavior is more common to add-on exporters and other third-party exporters.

Concentric and planar shading are defined in this text for sake of example. While not by any means equivalent, similar problems can occur when *smooth shading* and *flat shading* are misused, respectively. Smooth shading refers to creating a single normal per vertex using a composition of adjacent face normals, and flat shading refers to creating many normals per vertex using each individual face normal. In the case of a one-unit cube, concentric normals and smooth shading appear equivalent, and face normals and flat shading appear to be equivalent.

Figure 4-7. Planar normals (flat shading) in WebGL

This problem can be solved in a few ways depending on the specific exporter. In many cases, the target file format does not support face-level normals or *face normals*, so we must force Blender to work with vertex-level normals or *vertex normals*. In this case, we have Blender create multiple instances of each vertex, so that it can assign a separate normal to each. In our cube example, each vertex of a cube is connected to three separate faces, so needs three separate vertex normals.

We can use the Edge Split modifier to accomplish this. This can be found in **Properties ➤ Modifiers ➤ Add Modifier ➤ Edge Split**. Adjust the split threshold to your liking and choose **Apply**. See Listing 4-10 for a Blender Python method of accessing this modifier. This can easily be wrapped in a function and would fit well in the `ut.sel` function class established in previous chapters.

Listing 4-10. Cube with Planar Normals

```
# Add modifier to selected objects
bpy.ops.object.modifier_add(type='EDGE_SPLIT')

# Set split threshold in radians
bpy.context.object.modifiers["EdgeSplit"].split_angle = (3.1415 / 180) * 5

# Apply modifier
bpy.ops.object.modifier_apply(apply_as='DATA', modifier='EdgeSplit')
```

The result is shown to be very effective. Figures 4-8 and 4-9 show the before and after normal vectors viewed in Blender.

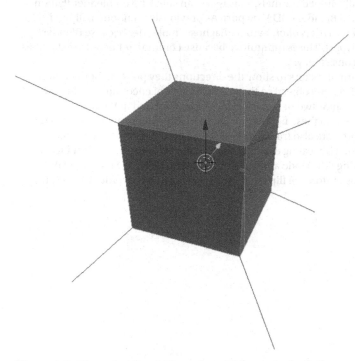

Figure 4-8. *Normal vectors before edge split (smooth shaded)*

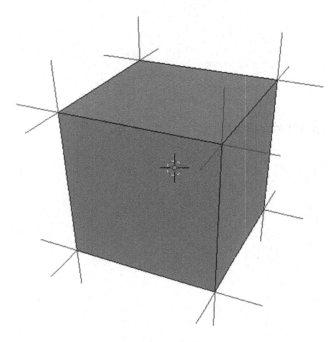

Figure 4-9. *Normal vectors after edge split (flat shaded)*

Flipped Normals

Another common problem is unintentionally flipped normals. This issue can sneak up on Blender Python programmers because of certain behaviors of Blender's 3D Viewport. As previously mentioned, flipped normals can make planes appear transparent. This is often hard to diagnose in Blender because Blender treats all planes as two-sided in the 3D Viewport. This is unintuitive because common renderers treat planes as one-sided for sake of performance and consistency.

In Figures 4-8 and 4-9, we drew the normal vectors to show the directions they point. In both of these figures, the normals clearly point outward from the object, so there is no danger of encountering flipped normals upon export. Figures 4-10 and 4-11 show two perspectives of a cube rendered in WebGL with flipped normals on a single face. As we can see in these figures, the face with flipped normals is transparent, and the faces we would expect to see behind it are also transparent because we are viewing them from behind. Mathematically, this can be remedied by scaling each flipped normal vector by –1. Within Blender, this can be performed fairly easily by entering Edit Mode and navigating to **Tool Shelf ➤ Shading / UVs ➤ Shading ➤ Normals ➤ Flip Direction**. This button will flip the normals of all selected, vertices, edges, or faces depending on the selected parts.

Figure 4-10. *Cube with flipped normals on single face (perspective #1)*

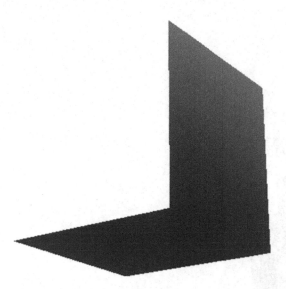

Figure 4-11. Cube with flipped normals on single face (perspective #2)

In Blender's Python API, we can perform the same function by calling bpy.ops.mesh.flip_normals() while in Edit Mode with some parts of the object selected. Complex procedural generation will often produce poorly oriented normals that can be corrected post-generation with this function.

The **Tool Shelf ➤ Shading / UVs ➤ Shading ➤ Normals ➤ Recalculate** command, which calls bpy.ops.mesh.normals_make_consistent(), will tell Blender to recalculate normals of well-defined objects to the best of its ability. This does not behave well for every object but can be useful nonetheless.

Z-Fighting

Z-fighting is a common rendering issue that produces glitchy objects without throwing errors or crashing the renderer. Most animators and gamers are familiar with this problem regardless of whether they have heard the term for it. See Figure 4-12 for an example of Z-fighting among four cubes in Blender in Rendered view.

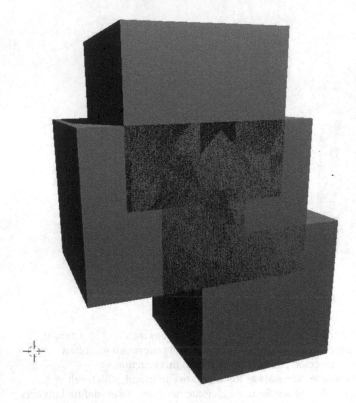

Figure 4-12. *Z-fighting of cubes with coplanar faces*

To understand why Z-fighting occurs, we must understand how *depth buffers* function in renderers. In almost every case, the computations involved in rendering an object occur on graphics processing units (GPUs) with very standardized graphics APIs (e.g., OpenGL and DirectX). The standard protocol in these rendering APIs is to use the camera's position relative to the meshes to determine which objects are visible and invisible to the user. This information is stored in the depth buffer. Before presenting a 2D image on the screen, the depth buffer tells the renderer which mesh pixel is closest to the camera and therefore visible to the user.

Given this information, why does the depth buffer not favor one mesh over another to prevent the glitchy Z-fighting effect? The depth buffer stores high-precision floating-point values, and renderers do not make adjustments to assess the equality of floating-point numbers. Low-level languages that drive graphics APIs maintain efficiency by making naive floating-point number comparisons. For the same reason that `0.1 * 0.1 > 0.01` returns `True` in Python, floating-point number comparisons behave inconsistently in renderers. The problems associated with floating-point arithmetic are well-studied in computer science, and floating-point equality is one of its most significant challenges.

How does one solve this problem given the tools in Blender and its Python API? There are a number of solutions, depending on the particular situation.

- Translate each object by a small and unnoticeable amount (around `0.000001` Blender units) such that the surfaces are no longer coplanar. If the translation has no effect, try translating it by a slightly larger distance.
- Delete interior faces in Edit Mode.
- Retool your algorithm to generate non-overlapping surfaces.
- Use the dissolve and limit dissolve tools in Edit Mode.

Ultimately, there are many methods for dealing with Z-fighting that all amount to making sure coplanar surfaces no longer exist in your model. We refrain from detailing all of the potential methods.

Conclusion

It is important to remember that Blender has abstracted away from many of the low-level 3D modeling concepts discussed here. It is helpful to us that we do not have to worry about data representations, shading semantics, and Z-fighting the vast majority of the time. We introduce these concepts nonetheless beacuse, when debugging, awareness of these issues and their drivers can prevent a lot of headache.

■ ■ ■

## CHAPTER 5

Introduction to Add-On Development

This chapter builds basic add-ons using using Blender's Python API. One of the biggest hurdles of add-on development is transitioning from a development environment to a neatly packaged and OS-independent add-on, so we spend considerable time in this chapter discussing various development practices. By the end of the chapter, readers should be able to register simple add-ons in both development and deployment environments. Following chapters build on this knowledge to incorporate more advanced features into add-ons.

A Simple Add-On Template

For this section, enter the scripting view in Blender and go to **Text Editor ➤ New** to create a new script. Give it a name, for example, `simpleaddon.py`. See Listing 5-1 for a simple template from where we can start building our add-on. Running this script will create a new tab in the Tools panel called "Simple Addon" that has a simple text input field and a button. The button will print a message to the console verifying that the plugin works, then parrot back the string in the text input field. See Figure 5-1 for the appearance and location of the add-on's GUI.

Listing 5-1. Simple Add-On Template

```
bl_info = {
    "name": "Simple Add-on Template",
    "author": "Chris Conlan",
    "location": "View3D > Tools > Simple Addon",
    "version": (1, 0, 0),
    "blender": (2, 7, 8),
    "description": "Starting point for new add-ons.",
    "wiki_url": "http://example.com",
    "category": "Development"
}

# Custom modules are imported here
# See end of chapter example for suggested protocol

import bpy
```

C. Conlan, *The Blender Python API*, DOI 10.1007/978-1-4842-2802-9_5

```python
# Panels, buttons, operators, menus, and
# functions are all declared in this area

# A simple Operator class

class SimpleOperator(bpy.types.Operator):
    bl_idname = "object.simple_operator"
    bl_label = "Print an Encouraging Message"

    def execute(self, context):
        print("\n\n################################################")
        print("# Add-on and Simple Operator executed successfully!")
        print("# " + context.scene.encouraging_message)
        print("################################################")
        return {'FINISHED'}

    @classmethod
    def register(cls):
        print("Registered class: %s " % cls.bl_label)

        # Register properties related to the class here
        bpy.types.Scene.encouraging_message = bpy.props.StringProperty(
            name="",
            description="Message to print to user",
            default="Have a nice day!")

    @classmethod
    def unregister(cls):
        print("Unregistered class: %s " % cls.bl_label)

        # Delete parameters related to the class here
        del bpy.types.Scene.encouraging_message

# A simple button and input field in the Tools panel
class SimplePanel(bpy.types.Panel):
    bl_space_type = "VIEW_3D"
    bl_region_type = "TOOLS"
    bl_category = "Simple Addon"
    bl_label = "Call Simple Operator"
    bl_context = "objectmode"

    def draw(self, context):
        self.layout.operator("object.simple_operator",
                             text="Print Encouraging Message")
        self.layout.prop(context.scene, 'encouraging_message')

    @classmethod
    def register(cls):
        print("Registered class: %s " % cls.bl_label)
        # Register properties related to the class here.
```

```python
    @classmethod
    def unregister(cls):
        print("Unregistered class: %s " % cls.bl_label)
        # Delete parameters related to the class here

def register():

    # Implicitly register objects inheriting bpy.types in current file and scope
    #bpy.utils.register_module(__name__)

    # Or explicitly register objects
    bpy.utils.register_class(SimpleOperator)
    bpy.utils.register_class(SimplePanel)

    print("%s registration complete\n" % bl_info.get('name'))

def unregister():

    # Always unregister in reverse order to prevent error due to
    # interdependencies

    # Explicitly unregister objects
    # bpy.utils.unregister_class(SimpleOperator)
    # bpy.utils.unregister_class(SimplePanel)

    # Or unregister objects inheriting bpy.types in current file and scope
    bpy.utils.unregister_module(__name__)
    print("%s unregister complete\n" % bl_info.get('name'))

# Only called during development with 'Text Editor -> Run Script'
# When distributed as plugin, Blender will directly
# and call register() and unregister()
if __name__ == "__main__":

    try:
        unregister()
    except Exception as e:
        # Catch failure to unregister explicitly
        print(e)
        pass

    register()
```

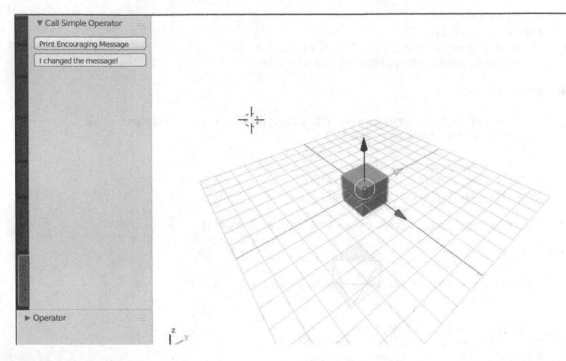

Figure 5-1. *Simple add-on template*

When we run the script, we should get console output about the registration and unregistration of the classes we declared in Listing 5-1. By changing the messages and choosing Print Encouraging Message, we should get something like the following in the console:

```
Unregistered class: Print an Encouraging Message
Unregistered class: Call Simple Operator
Simple Add-on Template unregister complete

Registered class: Print an Encouraging Message
Registered class: Call Simple Operator
Simple Add-on Template registration complete


##################################################
# Add-on and Simple Operator executed successfully!
# Have a nice day!
##################################################

##################################################
# Add-on and Simple Operator executed successfully!
# I changed the message!
##################################################
```

Though there are many specifics to explain, Blender add-ons are fairly elegant and readable. While every line of code has a purpose, the scripts benefit from consistency via repetition. The template presented in Figure 5-1 is fairly minimal, but we also included a handful of optional quality controls. We discuss each component before proceeding to more advanced add-ons.

Components of Blender Add-Ons

Blender add-ons rely on many different and specifically named variables and class functions to operate properly. We detail them by category here.

The bl_info Dictionary

The first thing to appear in a Blender add-on should be the bl_info dictionary. This dictionary is parsed from the first 1024 bytes of the source file so it is imperative that bl_info appear at the top of the file. We will use the word *dictionary* to refer to Python objects of class dict in writing.

Blender's internal engine uses data in this dictionary to populate various metadata related to the add-on itself. If we navigate to **Header Menu ➤ File ➤ User Preferences ➤ Add-ons**, we can see various official and community add-ons already in Blender. Clicking the caret on any of the add-ons shows how bl_info information is used to populate this GUI, as shown in Figure 5-2.

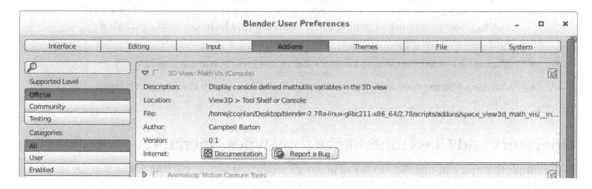

Figure 5-2. *How Blender uses bl_info*

It is important to note that the bl_info dictionary does not have any functional bearing on the add-on, rather it determines how the eventual user can find and activate it in this window. See the detailed description here:

- *name*—The name of the plugin as it appears in the add-ons tab of the user preferences (e.g., Math Vis (Console), Motion Capture Tools). It is written as a single string.

- *author*—The Name of the author or authors as it appears in the user preferences (e.g., Campbell Barton, Fabian Fricke). It can be a string with commas or a tuple of strings.

- *location*—The primary location of the add-on's GUI. Common syntax is **Window ➤ Panel ➤ Tab ➤ Section** for add-ons in the Tools, Properties, and Toolshelf panels. When in doubt, follow conventions established by other add-ons.

- *version*—The version number of the add-on as a tuple.

- *blender*—According to the Blender Wiki, this is the minimum Blender version number required to run the add-on. Community add-ons often falsely list (2, 7, 8) as the version when lower versions can support an add-on. In many cases the number refers the minimum version the developer has chosen to support.

- *description*—A brief description that appears in the user preferences window specified as a single string.

- *wiki_url*—An URL pointing to the handbook or guide for the add-on specified as a single string.

- *category*—A string specifying one the categories listed in Table 5-1.

Table 5-1. *The bl-info Category Options*

3D View	Compositing	Lighting	Object	Rigging	Text Editor
Add Mesh	Development	Material	Paint	Scene	UV
Add Curve	Game Engine	Mesh	Physics	Sequencer	User Interface
Animation	Import-Export	Node	Render	System	

There are a few remaining bl_info options that are less often seen.

- *support*—OFFICIAL, COMMUNITY, or TESTING. Where *official* refers to officially supported Blender add-ons, *community* refers community-supported add-ons, and *testing* refers to unfinished or new add-ons that should be intentionally excluded from Blender releases.

- *tracker_url*—URL pointing to a bug tracker (e.g., GitHub issues or similar).

- *warning*—String specifying some warning that will appear in the user preferences window.

Operators and Class Inheritance (bpy.types.Operator)

In the simplest sense, add-ons allow us to call Blender Python functions by clicking a button in the standard Blender GUI. Functions called by the Blender GUI must first be registered as operators of class bpy.types. Operator. Take for example SimpleOperator. When we register this class, the call to SimpleOperator. execute() is mapped to a function object in bpy.ops. The function is bpy.ops that it is mapped to is determined by the bl_idname value at the head of the class. Thus, after you run the script in Listing 5-1, you can print an encouraging message by calling bpy.ops.object.simple_operator() from the Interactive Console, from the add-on itself, or from unrelated Python scripts.

The following are the steps to declare an operator in Blender. Refer to the SimpleOperator class definition in Listing 5-1 throughout.

1. Declare a class that inherits bpy.types.Operator. This will appear in our code as:

   class MyNewOperator(bpy.types.Operator):

2. Declare bl_idname as a string with class and function name of your choice, separated by a period (e.g., object.simple_operator or simple.message). The class and function names can only contain lowercase characters and underscores. The execute function will later be accessible at bpy.ops.my_bl_idname.

3. (Optional) Declare a bl_label as any string describing the function of the class. This will appear in function documentation and metadata automatically generated by Blender.

4. Declare an execute function. This function will act as a normal class function and will always accept a reference to `bpy.context` as a parameter. By design of the `bpy.types.Operator` class, the execute function will always be defined as:

```
def execute(self, context):
```

It is best practice to return `{"FINISHED"}` for a successful call to `execute()` within an operator class.

5. (Optional) Declare class methods for registering and unregistering the class. The `register` and `unregister` functions will always require the `@classmethod` decorator and take `cls` as an argument. These functions are run whenever Blender attempts to register or unregister the operator class. It is helpful during development to include a print statement about class registration and deregistration as we have done in Listing 5-1 to check that Blender is not mistakenly reregistering existing classes. It is also important to note that we can declare and delete *scene properties* in these functions. We discuss this in later sections.

There are a handful of restrictions and guidelines to follow to ensure Blender can use our Python code. Ultimately, these guidelines change the way we code and the way we think about architecting Python codebases. This is the point in our understanding of the Blender Python API where it starts to feel like a true *application programming interface* (API) rather than just a collection of useful functions.

Panels and Class Inheritance (bpy.types.Panel)

The `bpy.types.Panel` class is next most common class inherited in add-ons. Panels already make up the majority of Blender's Tools, Toolshelf, and Properties windows. Each collapsible section of one of these windows is a distinct panel. For example, if we navigate to **3D Viewport ➤ Tools ➤ Tools** we see three panels by default: Transform, Edit, and History. Within a Blender Python add-on, these would be represented by three distinct `bpy.types.Panel` classes.

Here are the requirements to register a panel. Reference the `SimplePanel` class in Listing 5-1 throughout.

1. Declare a class that inherits `bpy.types.Panel`. This will appear as `class MyNewPanel(bpy.types.Panel):`.

2. Declare `bl_space_type`, `bl_region_type`, `bl_category`, and `bl_label`. Readers may have noticed the ordering of these is intentional (though not necessary). These four variables, in the order written and in Listing 5-1, specify the path that the user takes to reach the panel. In Listing 5-1, this reads **VIEW_3D ➤ TOOLS ➤ Simple Addon ➤ Call Simple Operator**, which looks very familiar to the way we have located GUI elements thus far in the text. Correct case and spelling matter in these variables. While the category and label can be arbitrary values, the space and region must reference real areas of the Blender GUI. See Tables 5-2 and 5-3 for the list of possible arguments to `bl_space_type` and `bl_region_type`.

Table 5-2. *bl-space-type Options*

EMPTY	NLA_EDITOR	NODE_EDITOR	INFO
VIEW_3D	IMAGE_EDITOR	LOGIC_EDITOR	FILE_BROWSER
TIMELINE	SEQUENCE_EDITOR	PROPERTIES	CONSOLE
GRAPH_EDITOR	CLIP_EDITOR	OUTLINER	
DOPESHEET_EDITOR	TEXT_EDITOR	USER_PREFERENCES	

Table 5-3. *bl-region-type Options*

WINDOW	HEADER	CHANNELS	TEMPORARY UI	TOOLS	TOOL_PROPS	PREVIEW

Most combinations of bl_space_type and bl_region_type do not work together, but logical combinations will generally work. There is presently no complete documentation on which space types and region types cooperate. Also, not all space types and region types require a declaration of bl_category or bl_label. Again, using them where logical typically gives good results.

3. (Optional) Declare bl_context. As in the previous example, we can set bl_context equal to objectmode to make the panel only appear in Object Mode. As of the time of writing, we do not have a concrete list of valid options for this variable. The API documentation currently has a TODO tag requesting more explanation. We introduce in a later chapter the poll() method, which is a much more flexible way of implementing this type of behavior.

4. Declare the draw method. This function takes the context as a parameter and will always be declared as def draw(self, context):. In this function definition, it is important to note that context refers to the bpy.context object but should not be passed as bpy.context. The important variables in the body of this function are bpy.context.scene and self.layout. The layout.prop() function can reference scene properties, object properties, and a few other Blender internal properties. It will automatically create the appropriate input field based on the scene property itself. The encouraging_message scene property in Listing 5-1 was declared as a string property, so supplying it as an argument to layout. prop() produced a text entry field. The layout.operator() function takes the bl_idname of an operator and creates a button with label specified by the text = argument. We will not go into detail about the layout object here, because it can get very complex for advanced GUIs. We discuss the layout object in detail later in this chapter.

5. (Optional) Declare register() and unregister() functions with decorator @classmethod, as in our discussion of bpy.types.Operator classes.

Register() and Unregister()

Near the end of Listing 5-1 are two functions, register() and unregister(), that are required in add-ons. These two functions are responsible for calling bpy.utils.register_class(), bpy.utils.unregister_ class(), bpy.utils.register_module(), and bpy.utils.unregister_module(). Any class that inherits a bpy.type class needs to be registered for it to be used by Blender in the add-on. Blender uses the unregister() function when an add-on is switched off by the user in the user preferences.

We have two choices for registering and unregistering classes. Some work better than others for development and others work better for deployment.

- Explicitly register and unregister each class. In this case, we want to register classes in a logical sequence. Classes that depend on others should be registered after their dependents. We do this in the register() function using bpy.utils.register_ class(), passing the class name as an argument. The classes should be unregistered in reverse order using bpy.utils.unregister_class() in the unregister() function.

- Implicitly register and unregister classes according to its membership in a module. We do so with the bpy.utils.register_module() and bpy.utils.unregister_ module() functions. We often see bpy.utils.register_module(__name__) called in the register() function of published add-ons, but it can be messy during development, as we explain shortly.

Looking back at Listing 5-1, we see that we have explicitly registered but implicitly unregistered our classes. This setup is, in the author's opinion, ideal for live editing of single-file add-ons. The bpy.utils. unregister_module(__name__) works as intended to clear the add-on environment of classes registered in previous runs of the script. During editing done using Blender's Text Editor, bpy.utils.register_module (__name__) often registers dead or unused copies of classes from previous runs of the script.

Therefore, the *clean slate* approach to live editing add-ons seems to be explicitly registering and implicitly deregistering. Implicit deregistration will pick up stray class instances from previous runs, then explicit registration instantiates only the newly created classes from the current run. This goes against the advice of most documentation, which typically suggests registering and deregistering using one of the styles in Listing 5-2. Our methods in Listing 5-1 are safe, verbose, and can be easily modified to conform to the commonly accepted practices in Listing 5-2.

Listing 5-2. Registration Protocol

```
# Option 1:
# Using implicit registration

def register():
    bpy.utils.register_module(__name__)

def unregister():
    bpy.utils.unregister_module(__name__)

if __name__ == "__main__":
    register()

# Option 2:
# Using explicit registration

def register():
    bpy.utils.register_class(SimpleOperator)
    bpy.utils.register_class(SimplePanel)

def unregister():
    bpy.utils.unregister_class(SimpleOperator)
    bpy.utils.unregister_class(SimplePanel)
```

```
if __name__ == "__main__":
    register()

# Option 3 (Recommended)
# Explicit registration and implicit unregistration
# With safe + verbose single-script run

def register():
    bpy.utils.register_class(SimpleOperator)
    bpy.utils.register_class(SimplePanel)

def unregister():
    bpy.utils.unregister_module(__name__)

if __name__ == "__main__":
    try:
        unregister()
    except Exception as e:
        print(e)
        pass

    register()
```

Scene Properties and bpy.props

Properties that are added to the Scene and Object types will be saved to the .blend file. In order for users to modify variables via the Blender GUI, they must be registered as bpy.props.* objects. The bpy.props class has options for most data types, including floats, integers, strings, and Booleans. They may be registered to bpy.types.* classes, including Scene and Object. In this section, we discuss how to register simple scene properties to bpy.types.Scene.* variables. These are arbitrarily named variables that are accessible via bpy.context.scene.*. While the name is arbitrary, it is restricted to lowercase characters and underscores.

There are two places we can register scene variables:

- In the register() function at the bottom of the script.

- In the register() classmethod of any class that inherits a bpy.types.* class (panels, operators, menus, etc.).

Most commonly, scene variables are tied directly to a class. For sake of clarity and organization, we want to declare those variables within the register() classmethod of that class. Other variables that do not fit neatly into a class definition can be declared in the register() function at the bottom of the script. In this text, we encourage that scene properties are declared in the register() classmethod if closely associated with a specific class, but this is not commonly seen in existing community add-ons.

Scene variables will be instances of bpy.types.* variables. These include the Blender types StringProperty, FloatProperty, IntProperty, and BoolProperty. Any time a panel includes a variable in a GUI via a call to self.layout.prop, the variable will be logically formatted according to its type. Integers and floats appear in slider bars, strings appear as text input fields, Booleans appear as checkboxes, and so on.

In Listing 5-3, we redeclare SimpleOperator and SimplePanel from Listing 5-1 with additional scene variables. Readers will rewrite these classes using Listing 5-1 as a template. See Figure 5-3 for the resulting GUI.

Listing 5-3. Exploring Scene Properties

```python
# Simple Operator with Extra Properties
class SimpleOperator(bpy.types.Operator):
    bl_idname = "object.simple_operator"
    bl_label = "Print an Encouraging Message"

    def execute(self, context):
        print("\n\n#################################################")
        print("# Add-on and Simple Operator executed successfully!")
        print("# Encouraging Message:", context.scene.encouraging_message)
        print("# My Int:", context.scene.my_int_prop)
        print("# My Float:", context.scene.my_float_prop)
        print("# My Bool:", context.scene.my_bool_prop)
        print("# My Int Vector:", *context.scene.my_int_vector_prop)
        print("# My Float Vector:", *context.scene.my_float_vector_prop)
        print("# My Bool Vector:", *context.scene.my_bool_vector_prop)
        print("#################################################")
        return {'FINISHED'}

    @classmethod
    def register(cls):
        print("Registered class: %s " % cls.bl_label)

        bpy.types.Scene.encouraging_message = bpy.props.StringProperty(
            name="",
            description="Message to print to user",
            default="Have a nice day!")

        bpy.types.Scene.my_int_prop = bpy.props.IntProperty(
            name="My Int",
            description="Sample integer property to print to user",
            default=123,
            min=100,
            max=200)

        bpy.types.Scene.my_float_prop = bpy.props.FloatProperty(
            name="My Float",
            description="Sample float property to print to user",
            default=3.1415,
            min=0.0,
            max=10.0,
            precision=4)

        bpy.types.Scene.my_bool_prop = bpy.props.BoolProperty(
            name="My Bool",
            description="Sample boolean property to print to user",
            default=True)
```

```python
        bpy.types.Scene.my_int_vector_prop = bpy.props.IntVectorProperty(
            name="My Int Vector",
            description="Sample integer vector property to print to user",
            default=(1, 2, 3, 4),
            subtype='NONE',
            size=4)

        bpy.types.Scene.my_float_vector_prop = bpy.props.FloatVectorProperty(
            name="My Float Vector",
            description="Sample float vector property to print to user",
            default=(1.23, 2.34, 3.45),
            subtype='XYZ',
            size=3,
            precision=2)

        bpy.types.Scene.my_bool_vector_prop = bpy.props.BoolVectorProperty(
            name="My Bool Vector",
            description="Sample bool vector property to print to user",
            default=(True, False, True),
            subtype='XYZ',
            size=3)

    @classmethod
    def unregister(cls):
        print("Unregistered class: %s " % cls.bl_label)
        del bpy.types.Scene.encouraging_message

# Simple button in Tools panel
class SimplePanel(bpy.types.Panel):
    bl_space_type = "VIEW_3D"
    bl_region_type = "TOOLS"
    bl_category = "Simple Addon"
    bl_label = "Call Simple Operator"
    bl_context = "objectmode"

    def draw(self, context):
        self.layout.operator("object.simple_operator",
                             text="Print Encouraging Message")
        self.layout.prop(context.scene, 'encouraging_message')
        self.layout.prop(context.scene, 'my_int_prop')
        self.layout.prop(context.scene, 'my_float_prop')
        self.layout.prop(context.scene, 'my_bool_prop')
        self.layout.prop(context.scene, 'my_int_vector_prop')
        self.layout.prop(context.scene, 'my_float_vector_prop')
        self.layout.prop(context.scene, 'my_bool_vector_prop')

    @classmethod
    def register(cls):
        print("Registered class: %s " % cls.bl_label)
        # Register properties related to the class here.

    @classmethod
    def unregister(cls):
        print("Unregistered class: %s " % cls.bl_label)
```

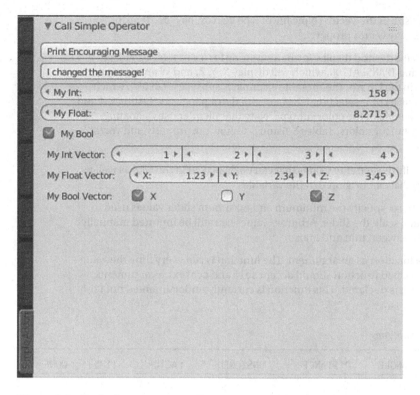

Figure 5-3. *Exploring scene properties*

See Table 5-4 for a list of available bpy.props.* variables. See the API documentation page for bpy.props for more information. So far we have not covered EnumProperty, CollectionProperty, or PointerProperty. We cover EnumProperty later in this chapter, and we cover CollectionProperty in Chapter 7 on advanced add-on functionalities.

Table 5-4. *Available Blender Properties*

BoolProperty	EnumProperty	IntProperty	StringProperty
BoolVectorProperty	FloatProperty	IntVectorProperty	
CollectionProperty	FloatVectorProperty	PointerProperty	

The arguments given to property declarations are generally straightforward, and many of them are shared across different properties. Most notably:

- default= is a value or tuple of a length equal to the size that specifies the default value.

- name= is the value that will appear in the GUI to the left of the input field.

- description= is a character string that is displayed when the user hovers his cursor over the GUI element.

- precision= specifies the decimal precision in the display of any float property.

- `size=` specifies the size of the vector (typically of type `Vector`, `bpy_boolean`, or `bpy_int`) desired in any vector property.

- `subtype=` specifies the desired display formatting string for a variable. Useful examples are `XYZ` and `TRANSLATION`, which will display X, Y, Z, and W ahead of your first four variables in the UI. Another notable example is `subtype="COLOR"`, which will create an attractive color selection UI when added to a panel. See Listing 5-4 and Figure 5-4 for an example of the color subtype. Note that Blender uses a floating-point range of (0.0, 1.0) for colors. Tables 5-5 and 5-6 show the property and vector property subtypes.

- `min=` and `max=` specify the extreme values that can be displayed in the GUI as well as the extreme values that can be stored in the variables.

- `softmin=` and `softmax=` specify the minimum and maximum slider values used to display variables and scale the slider. Arbitrary values can still be inputted manually so long as they are between min and max.

- `update=` accepts a function as an argument. The function is run every time the value is updated. The specified function should accept `self` and `context` as arguments regardless of where it is declared. This function is currently undocumented but fairly well-behaved.

Table 5-5. *Available Property Subtypes*

PIXEL	PERCENTAGE	ANGLE	DISTANCE	UNSIGNED	FACTOR	TIME	NONE

Table 5-6. *Available Vector Property Subtypes*

COLOR	VELOCITY	EULER	XYZ	NONE
TRANSLATION	ACCELERATION	QUATERNION	COLOR_GAMMA	
DIRECTION	MATRIX	AXISANGLE	LAYER	

Listing 5-4. Using the Color Subtype

```
bpy.types.Scene.my_color_prop = bpy.props.FloatVectorProperty(
    name="My Color Property",
    description="Returns a vector of length 4",
    default=(0.322, 1.0, 0.182, 1.0),
    min=0.0,
    max=1.0,
    subtype='COLOR',
    size=4)
```

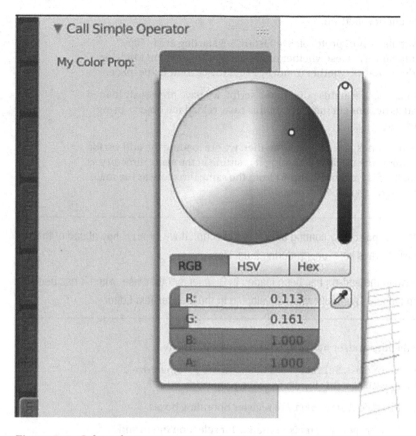

Figure 5-4. Color subtype

Precision Selection Add-On Example

At this point in the text, we have discussed Blender Python API concepts in a sufficient capacity to start building effective add-ons. For our first real add-on, we will parameterize the ut.act.select_by_loc() function declared in Chapter 3 to enable precise group selection in Edit Mode.

Before we begin, make sure to download Chapter 3's iteration of ut.py from http://blender. chrisconlan.com/ut.py. We will import this in our add-on. The community has used a few different protocols for managing custom imports in add-ons. We will discuss a common protocol for managing custom imports from single-level directories. In other words, we will import custom modules that lie in the same directory as the main script.

Code Overview for Our Add-On

We outline the steps taken to build the add-on, from development through deployment and sharing:

1. Create the main script and name it __init__.py in Blender's Text Editor. Copy the add-on template from Listing 5-1 into this script.

2. Create a second script and name it ut.py in Blender's Text Editor. Copy the Python module at http://blender.chrisconlan.com/ut.py into this script.

3. Modify `bl_info` for our new add-on.

4. Add the custom module import protocol. See Listing 5-5 starting at `if "bpy"` `in locals():`. Quite simply, to test whether or not we are Deployment Mode or Development Mode, we check whether or not bpy is in the current namespace.

   - If bpy is in the namespace at this point in the script, we have previously loaded the add-on and its dependent modules. In this case, reload the objects using `importlib.reload()`.

   - If bpy is not in the namespace at this point, then we are loading the add-on for the first time. Import the module assuming it is sitting in the same directory as `__init__.py` in the filesystem. To import from the same directory as the main script, we use `from . import custommodule`.

■ **Note** This protocol depends on `import bpy` coming after it in the script. If we `import bpy` ahead of this protocol, then bpy in `locals()` will always be `True`, rendering it useless.

This protocol will behave nicely when the add-on has been loaded in Blender, or otherwise, when it has been deployed. We will import custom modules normally when developing in the Blender Text Editor.

---

5. Import any native Blender and/or native Python modules normally.

6. Declare our core operator class, `SelectByLocation`. We will parameterize `ut.` `act.select_by_loc()` with sensible inputs as scene properties.

   - Use `bpy.props.FloatVectorProperty` to register bounding boxes.

   - Use `bpy.props.EnumProperty` to register menus for selection mode and coordinate system. See Listings 3-8 through 3-10 in Chapter 3 for an explanation of these parameters.

7. Declare our core panel class, `XYZSelect`. We will organize the buttons and parameters associated with operator here. The default menu layout looks pretty intuitive in this case. Declare the `poll()` classmethod to return `True` only if the mode is Edit Mode.

8. Implement safe and verbose registration, as shown in Listing 5-1.

Listing 5-5. XYZ-Select Add-On

```
bl_info = {
    "name": "XYZ-Select",
    "author": "Chris Conlan",
    "location": "View3D > Tools > XYZ-Select",
    "version": (1, 0, 0),
    "blender": (2, 7, 8),
    "description": "Precision selection in Edit Mode",
    "category": "3D View"
}
```

```python
### Use these imports to during development ###
import ut
import importlib
importlib.reload(ut)

### Use these imports to package and ship your add-on ###
# if "bpy" in locals():
#     import importlib
#     importlib.reload(ut)
#     print('Reloaded ut.py')
# else:
#     from . import ut
#     print('Imported ut.py')

import bpy
import os
import random


# Simple Operator with Extra Properties

class xyzSelect(bpy.types.Operator):
    bl_idname = "object.xyz_select"
    bl_label = "Select pieces of objects in Edit Mode with bounding boxes"

    def execute(self, context):

        scn = context.scene

        output = ut.act.select_by_loc(lbound=scn.xyz_lower_bound,
                                      ubound=scn.xyz_upper_bound,
                                      select_mode=scn.xyz_selection_mode,
                                      oords=scn.xyz_coordinate_system)

        print("Selected " + str(output) + " " + scn.xyz_selection_mode + "s")

        return {'FINISHED'}

    @classmethod
    def register(cls):
        print("Registered class: %s " % cls.bl_label)
        bpy.types.Scene.xyz_lower_bound = bpy.props.FloatVectorProperty(
            name="Lower",
            description="Lower bound of selection bounding box",
            default=(0.0, 0.0, 0.0),
            subtype='XYZ',
            size=3,
            precision=2
        )
```

```python
        bpy.types.Scene.xyz_upper_bound = bpy.props.FloatVectorProperty(
            name="Upper",
            description="Upper bound of selection bounding box",
            default=(1.0, 1.0, 1.0),
            subtype='XYZ',
            size=3,
            precision=2
        )

        # Menus for EnumProperty's
        selection_modes = [
            ("VERT", "Vert", "", 1),
            ("EDGE", "Edge", "", 2),
            ("FACE", "Face", "", 3),
        ]
        bpy.types.Scene.xyz_selection_mode = \
            bpy.props.EnumProperty(items=selection_modes, name="Mode")

        coordinate_system = [
            ("GLOBAL", "Global", "", 1),
            ("LOCAL", "Local", "", 2),
        ]
        bpy.types.Scene.xyz_coordinate_system = \
            bpy.props.EnumProperty(items=coordinate_system, name="Coords")

    @classmethod
    def unregister(cls):
        print("Unregistered class: %s " % cls.bl_label)
        del bpy.context.scene.xyz_coordinate_system
        del bpy.context.scene.xyz_selection_mode
        del bpy.context.scene.xyz_upper_bound
        del bpy.context.scene.xyz_lower_bound


# Simple button in Tools panel
class xyzPanel(bpy.types.Panel):
    bl_space_type = "VIEW_3D"
    bl_region_type = "TOOLS"
    bl_category = "XYZ-Select"
    bl_label = "Select by Bounding Box"

    @classmethod
    def poll(self, context):
        return context.object.mode == 'EDIT'
```

```python
    def draw(self, context):
        scn = context.scene
        lay = self.layout
        lay.operator('object.xyz_select', text="Select Components")
        lay.prop(scn, 'xyz_lower_bound')
        lay.prop(scn, 'xyz_upper_bound')
        lay.prop(scn, 'xyz_selection_mode')
        lay.prop(scn, 'xyz_coordinate_system')

    @classmethod
    def register(cls):
        print("Registered class: %s " % cls.bl_label)

    @classmethod
    def unregister(cls):
        print("Unregistered class: %s " % cls.bl_label)

def register():
    # bpy.utils.register_module(__name__)

    bpy.utils.register_class(xyzSelect)
    bpy.utils.register_class(xyzPanel)

    print("%s registration complete\n" % bl_info.get('name'))

def unregister():
    # bpy.utils.unregister_class(xyzPanel)
    # bpy.utils.unregister_class(xyzSelect)

    bpy.utils.unregister_module(__name__)
    print("%s unregister complete\n" % bl_info.get('name'))

if __name__ == "__main__":
    try:
        unregister()
    except Exception as e:
        print(e)
        pass

    register()
```

See Figure 5-5 for an example of precisely contorting an icosphere using this plugin.

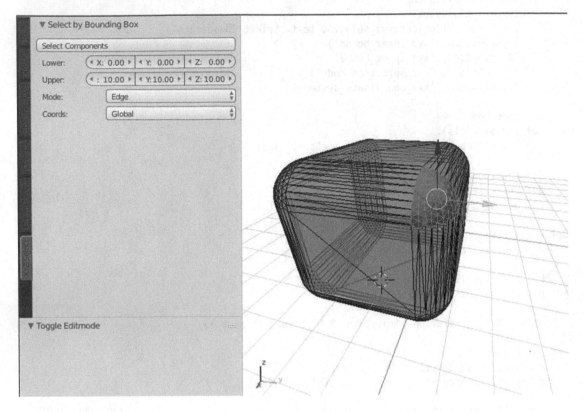

Figure 5-5. *Color subtype*

We introduced two new concepts in this example—the poll() classmethod and the EnumProperty variable. We explain these both next.

The poll() Classmethod

The poll() classmethod is a function typically placed after the bl_* variables in a panel declaration. The function will be called whenever the 3D Viewport updates to determine whether or not to display the panel.

If the function returns any non-null value, the panel will display. It is considered best practice to return a Boolean even though any non-null will suffice. Recall that the number 0, empty strings, and False are all considered null in Python.

In our add-on, we simply return True if the user is in Edit Mode, as seen here:

```python
# poll function for edit-mode-only panels
@classmethod
def poll(self, context):
    return context.object.mode == 'EDIT'
```

EnumProperty Variables

The bpy.props.EnumProperty class is how we display drop-down menus via API. It is instantiated by a list of tuples, where each element in a tuple represents a Blender data value. The schema is as follows:

```
my_enum_list = [
    ("python_1", "display_1", "tooltip_1", "icon_1", 'number_1),
    ("python_2", "display_2", "tooltip_2", "icon_2", 'number_2),
    # etc ...
    ("python_n", "display_n", "tooltip_n", "icon_n", 'number_n)
]
```

This is directly from the API documentation:

1. The first parameter is the value returned by bpy.context.scene.my_enum_list in Python.

2. The second parameter is the value displayed in the GUI menu.

3. The third value is the tooltip displayed in the GUI menu. It can be an empty string.

4. (Optional) Integer or string identifier, used internally and by bpy.types. UILayout.icon.

5. (Optional) Unique value stored in file data, used when the first parameter is potentially dynamic.

Preparing Our Add-On for Distribution

To prepare our add-on for distribution, follow these steps:

1. Uncomment the import lines per the instructions in the comments.

2. Revert script to explicit registration and explicit unregistration.

3. (Optional) Remove verbose print statements when you're done testing the add-on. This is purely to avoid cluttering the end user's terminal.

4. Replace the modules in the following file hierarchy and compress it as a .zip file.

```
xyz-select/
 |  __init__.py
 \  ut.py
```

To install our add-on, navigate to **Header Menu ➤ File ➤ User Preferences ➤ Add-ons ➤ Install From File**. From there, check and uncheck the box to enable and disable the add-on. This will trigger the register() and unregister() methods in __init__.py. Registration should succeed without errors.

To download the zipped add-on directly, go to http://blender.chrisconlan.com/xyz-select.zip.

Conclusion

In the next chapter, we discuss the blf and bgl modules for visualizing data in the 3D Viewport. In Chapter 7, we introduce advanced add-on development concepts.

CHAPTER 6

■ ■ ■

The bgl and blf Modules

The bgl module is a wrapper for OpenGL functions commonly used by Blender in the 3D Viewport and Blender Game Engine. OpenGL (Open Graphics Library) is an open source low-level API used in innumerable 3D applications to take advantage of hardware-accelerated computing.

The bgl documentation will seem familiar to those reader already familiar with OpenGL. The bgl module itself is meant to mimic to call structure and frame-by-frame rendering style of OpenGL 2.1.

In reading through the bgl documentation, we notice many advanced concepts like buffer operations, face culling, and rasterization. Fortunately for Blender Python programmers, the 3D Viewport manages these operations already. We are more concerned with marking up the 3D Viewport with extra information to help the user understand his models. This chapter focuses primarily on drawing with bgl.

The blf module is a small set of functions for displaying text and drawing fonts. It is closely related to bgl and rarely mentioned in examples without it. Blender Python developers commonly combine the bgl and blf modules to make measurement tools, drawing lines with bgl and displaying their measurements with blf. We do just that in this chapter.

Note that these modules are commonly seen in examples with the bge (Blender Game Engine) module. We will not be working in Blender Game Engine, so these scripts will not run, and attempts to import bge will fail. We restrict our drawing to the 3D Viewport.

Note also that the bgl module is set to be replaced or majorly reconstructed in Blender 2.80+. It is likely this chapter will be the first due for an update after the release of this text.

Instantaneous Drawing

The bgl and blf modules cannot be taught in the same way that other Blender Python modules can. When a line or character is drawn on the 3D Viewport by either of these modules, it is only visible for a single frame. So, we cannot experiment with it in the Interactive Console like we have with other modules. Functions we execute in the Interactive Console may execute without error, but we will not be able to view the results in the 3D Viewport.

To effectively use the bgl and blf modules, we must use them within a handler function that is set to update at every frame change. Thus, we start with a handler example using non-OpenGL concepts.

Handlers Overview

This section gives examples of handlers using bpy.app.handlers. This is not the submodule we will ultimately use when dealing with bgl and blf, but it is instructive for learning about handlers in Blender.

© Chris Conlan 2017
C. Conlan, *The Blender Python API*, DOI 10.1007/978-1-4842-2802-9_6

Clock Example

Handlers are functions that are set to run every time an event occurs. To instantiate a handler, we declare a function, then add it to one of the possible lists of handlers in Blender. In Listing 6-1, we create a function that modifies the text of a text mesh with the current time. We then add the function to bpy.app.handlers. scene_update_pre to indicate that we would like it to run right before the 3D Viewport is updated and displayed.

The result is what appears to be a clock in the 3D Viewport. In actuality, it is a text mesh that is updating many times per second. This example is not safe or full-proof, but as long as we keep the object in the scene and named MyTextObj, we can add and edit other objects with the clock running in the background. See Figure 6-1 for the result.

■ **Note**   The behavior of the clock is not a documented behavior and may change with future releases of Blender. Specifically, Blender intends to change what they qualify as a frame change. Currently, frame changes seem to happen instantaneously and constantly.

The official Blender documentation gives examples where the only parameter passed to the handler is a dummy. Handler functions should be treated like traditional Python lambdas, with the exception that a single dummy argument is required as the first parameter. We pass the function itself rather than the output of the function, and a new unnamed instance of the function is created when it is passed. We cannot easily access this unnamed function after it is created for the handler.

Listing 6-1. Blender Clock Handler Example

```
import bpy
import datetime

# Clear the scene
bpy.ops.object.select_all(action='SELECT')
bpy.ops.object.delete()

# Create an object for our clock
bpy.ops.object.text_add(location=(0, 0, 0))
bpy.context.object.name = 'MyTextObj'

# Create a handler function
def tell_time(dummy):
    current_time = datetime.datetime.now().strftime('%H:%M:%S.%f')[:-3]
    bpy.data.objects['MyTextObj'].data.body = current_time

# Add to the list of handler functions "scene_update_pre"
bpy.app.handlers.scene_update_pre.append(tell_time)
```

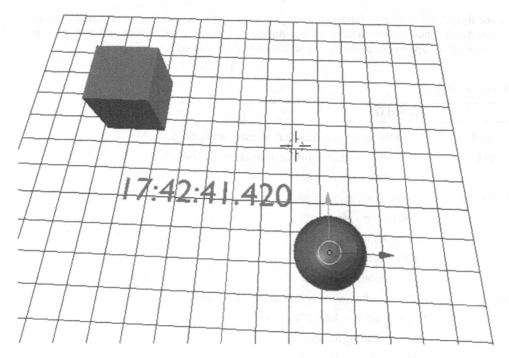

Figure 6-1. *Result of the Blender clock handler example*

Managing Handlers

In the case of bpy.app.handlers, we can edit various lists of functions to manage our handlers. These lists are quite literally Python classes of type list, and we can operate on them as such. We can use list class methods such as append(), pop(), remove(), and clear() to manage our handler functions. See Listing 6-2 for some useful examples.

Listing 6-2. Managing Handler Lists

```
# Will only work if 'tell_time' is in scope
bpy.app.handlers.scene_update_pre.remove(tell_time)

# Useful in development for a clean slate
bpy.app.handlers.scene_update_pre.clear()

# Remove handler at the end of the list and return it
bpy.app.handlers.scene_update_pre.pop()
```

Types of Handlers

In Listing 6-1, we used bpy.app.handlers.scene_update_pre to modify a mesh according to internal variables before each update. Table 6-1 details types of handlers in bpy.app.handlers as they appear in the official documentation.

There is some functional overlap in Table 6-1, and not every handler behaves how one would expect. For example, using `scene_update_post` in Listing 6-1 as opposed to `scene_update_pre` does not work at all. Readers are encouraged to experiment to determine which one fits their needs.

Table 6-1. *Types of Handlers*

Handler	Called On
`frame_change_post`	After frame change during rendering or playback
`frame_change_pre`	Before frame change during rendering or playback
`render_cancel`	Canceling a render job
`render_complete`	Completing a render job
`render_init`	Initializing a render job
`render_post`	After render
`render_pre`	Before render
`render_stats`	Printing render statistics
`render_write`	Directly after frame is written in rendering
`load_post`	After loading a .blend file
`load_pre`	Before loading a .blend file
`save_post`	After saving a .blend file
`save_pre`	Before saving a .blend file
`scene_update_post`	After updating scene data (e.g., 3D Viewport)
`scene_update_pre`	Before updating scene data (e.g. ,3D Viewport)
`game_pre`	Starting the game engine
`game_post`	Ending the game engine

Persistent Handlers

If we want handlers to persist after loading a `.blend` file, we can add the `@persistent` decorator. Normally, handlers are freed when loading a `.blend` file, so certain handlers like `bpy.app.handlers.load_post` necessitate this decorator. Listing 6-3 uses the `@persistent` decorator to print file diagnostics after loading a `.blend` file.

Listing 6-3. Printing File Diagnostics on Load

```
import bpy
from bpy.app.handlers import persistent

@persistent
def load_diag(dummy):
    obs = bpy.context.scene.objects
```

```
    print('\n\n### File Diagnostics ###')
    print('Objects in Scene:', len(obs))
    for ob in obs:
        print(ob.name, 'of type', ob.type)

bpy.app.handlers.load_post.append(load_diag)

# After reloading startup file:
#
# ### File Diagnostics ###
# Objects in Scene: 3
# Cube of type MESH
# Lamp of type LAMP
# Camera of type CAMERA
```

Handlers in blf and bgl

Now that we have a basic understanding of handlers, we will detail how to draw with OpenGL tools directly on the 3D Viewport. The handlers used for drawing on the 3D Viewport are not part of bpy.app.handlers, rather they are undocumented member functions of bpy.types.SpaceView3D. To understand these member functions, we have reduced real-world examples of their use by other developers.

Listing 6-4 shows how to use bgl and blf to draw the name of an object on its origin point.

Listing 6-4. Drawing the Name of an Object

```
import bpy
from bpy_extras import view3d_utils
import bgl
import blf

# Color and font size of text
rgb_label = (1, 0.8, 0.1, 1.0)
font_size = 16
font_id = 0

# Wrapper for mapping 3D Viewport to OpenGL 2D region

def gl_pts(context, v):
    return view3d_utils.location_3d_to_region_2d(
        context.region,
        context.space_data.region_3d,
        v)

# Get the active object, find its 2D points, draw the name

def draw_name(context):

    ob = context.object
    v = gl_pts(context, ob.location)

    bgl.glColor4f(*rgb_label)
```

```
    blf.size(font_id, font_size, 72)
    blf.position(font_id, v[0], v[1], 0)
    blf.draw(font_id, ob.name)

# Add the handler
# arguments:
# function = draw_name,
# tuple of parameters = (bpy.context,),
# constant1 = 'WINDOW',
# constant2 = 'POST_PIXEL'
bpy.types.SpaceView3D.draw_handler_add(
    draw_name, (bpy.context,), 'WINDOW', 'POST_PIXEL')
```

Running Listing 6-4 in the text editor will allow you to see the name of the active object drawn on its origin point.

Handlers created with bpy.types.SpaceView3D are not as easily accessible as those in bpy.app. handlers and are persistent by default. Unless we create better controls for flicking these handlers on and off, we will have to restart Blender to detach this handler. In the next section, we place this handler in an add-on that allows us to flick it on and off with a button. Also, we store the handler in a bpy.types.Operator so we will not lose our reference to the function after adding it to the handler.

■ **Note** The draw_handler_add() and draw_handler_remove() functions are currently undocumented in bpy.types.SpaceView3D in Blender's official documentation. Therefore, we will work with them as best we can based on known functional examples.

Example Add-On

This add-on is a standalone script, so it may be run by copying it into the Text Editor or importing it via the User Preferences. Readers are encouraged to run it via the Text Editor for easy experimentation. See Listing 6-5 for the add-on and Figure 6-2 for a screenshot of the result (in Edit Mode).

Listing 6-5. Simple Line and Text Drawing

```
bl_info = {
    "name": "Simple Line and Text Drawing",
    "author": "Chris Conlan",
    "location": "View3D > Tools > Drawing",
    "version": (1, 0, 0),
    "blender": (2, 7, 8),
    "description": "Minimal add-on for line and text drawing with bgl and blf. "
                   "Adapted from Antonio Vazquez's (antonioya) Archmesh." ,
    "wiki_url": "http://example.com",
    "category": "Development"
}

import bpy
import bmesh
import os
```

```python
import bpy_extras
import bgl
import blf

# view3d_utils must be imported explicitly
from bpy_extras import view3d_utils

def draw_main(self, context):
    """Main function, toggled by handler"""

    scene = context.scene
    indices = context.scene.gl_measure_indices

    # Set color and fontsize parameters
    rgb_line = (0.173, 0.545, 1.0, 1.0)
    rgb_label = (1, 0.8, 0.1, 1.0)
    fsize = 16

    # Enable OpenGL drawing
    bgl.glEnable(bgl.GL_BLEND)
    bgl.glLineWidth(1)

    # Store reference to active object
    ob = context.object

    # Draw vertex indices
    if scene.gl_display_verts:
        label_verts(context, ob, rgb_label, fsize)

    # Draw measurement
    if scene.gl_display_measure:
        if(indices[1] < len(ob.data.vertices)):
            draw_measurement(context, ob, indices, rgb_line, rgb_label, fsize)

    # Draw name
    if scene.gl_display_names:
        draw_name(context, ob, rgb_label, fsize)

    # Disable OpenGL drawings and restore defaults
    bgl.glLineWidth(1)
    bgl.glDisable(bgl.GL_BLEND)
    bgl.glColor4f(0.0, 0.0, 0.0, 1.0)

class glrun(bpy.types.Operator):
    """Main operator, flicks handler on/off"""

    bl_idname = "glinfo.glrun"
    bl_label = "Display object data"
    bl_description = "Display additional information in the 3D Viewport"

    # For storing function handler
    _handle = None
```

93

```
        # Enable GL drawing and add handler
        @staticmethod
        def handle_add(self, context):
            if glrun._handle is None:
                glrun._handle = bpy.types.SpaceView3D.draw_handler_add(
                    draw_main, (self, context), 'WINDOW', 'POST_PIXEL')
                context.window_manager.run_opengl = True

        # Disable GL drawing and remove handler
        @staticmethod
        def handle_remove(self, context):
            if glrun._handle is not None:
                bpy.types.SpaceView3D.draw_handler_remove(glrun._handle, 'WINDOW')
            glrun._handle = None
            context.window_manager.run_opengl = False

        # Flicks OpenGL handler on and off
        # Make sure to flick "off" before reloading script when live editing
        def execute(self, context):
            if context.area.type == 'VIEW_3D':

                if context.window_manager.run_opengl is False:
                    self.handle_add(self, context)
                    context.area.tag_redraw()
                else:
                    self.handle_remove(self, context)
                    context.area.tag_redraw()

                return {'FINISHED'}
            else:
                print("3D Viewport not found, cannot run operator.")
                return {'CANCELLED'}

class glpanel(bpy.types.Panel):
    """Standard panel with scene variables"""

    bl_idname = "glinfo.glpanel"
    bl_label = "Display Object Data"
    bl_space_type = 'VIEW_3D'
    bl_region_type = "TOOLS"
    bl_category = 'Drawing'

    def draw(self, context):
        lay = self.layout
        scn = context.scene

        box = lay.box()

        if context.window_manager.run_opengl is False:
            icon = 'PLAY'
            txt = 'Display'
```

```
    else:
        icon = 'PAUSE'
        txt = 'Hide'
    box.operator("glinfo.glrun", text=txt, icon=icon)

    box.prop(scn, "gl_display_names", toggle=True, icon="OUTLINER_OB_FONT")
    box.prop(scn, "gl_display_verts", toggle=True, icon='DOT')
    box.prop(scn, "gl_display_measure", toggle=True, icon="ALIGN")
    box.prop(scn, "gl_measure_indices")

@classmethod
def register(cls):

    bpy.types.Scene.gl_display_measure = bpy.props.BoolProperty(
        name="Measures",
        description="Display measurements for specified indices in active mesh.",
        default=True,
    )

    bpy.types.Scene.gl_display_names = bpy.props.BoolProperty(
        name="Names",
        description="Display names for selected meshes.",
        default=True,
    )

    bpy.types.Scene.gl_display_verts = bpy.props.BoolProperty(
        name="Verts",
        description="Display vertex indices for selected meshes.",
        default=True,
    )

    bpy.types.Scene.gl_measure_indices = bpy.props.IntVectorProperty(
        name="Indices",
        description="Display measurement between supplied vertices.",
        default=(0, 1),
        min=0,
        subtype='NONE',
        size=2)

    print("registered class %s " % cls.bl_label)

@classmethod
def unregister(cls):
    del bpy.types.Scene.gl_display_verts
    del bpy.types.Scene.gl_display_names
    del bpy.types.Scene.gl_display_measure
    del bpy.types.Scene.gl_measure_indices

    print("unregistered class %s " % cls.bl_label)
```

```python
##### Button-activated drawing functions #####

# Draw the name of the object on its origin
def draw_name(context, ob, rgb_label, fsize):
    a = gl_pts(context, ob.location)
    bgl.glColor4f(rgb_label[0], rgb_label[1], rgb_label[2], rgb_label[3])
    draw_text(a, ob.name, fsize)

# Draw line between two points, draw the distance
def draw_measurement(context, ob, pts, rgb_line, rgb_label, fsize):
    # pts = (index of vertex #1, index of vertex #2)

    a = coords(ob, pts[0])
    b = coords(ob, pts[1])

    d = dist(a, b)

    mp = midpoint(a, b)

    a = gl_pts(context, a)
    b = gl_pts(context, b)
    mp = gl_pts(context, mp)

    bgl.glColor4f(rgb_line[0], rgb_line[1], rgb_line[2], rgb_line[3]) draw_line(a, b)

    bgl.glColor4f(rgb_label[0], rgb_label[1], rgb_label[2], rgb_label[3])
    draw_text(mp, '%.3f' % d, fsize)

# Label all possible vertices of object
def label_verts(context, ob, rgb, fsize):
    try:
        # attempt get coordinates, will except if object does not have vertices
        v = coords(ob)
        bgl.glColor4f(rgb[0], rgb[1], rgb[2], rgb[3])
        for i in range(0, len(v)):
            loc = gl_pts(context, v[i])
            draw_text(loc, str(i), fsize)
    except AttributeError :
        # Except attribute error to not fail on lights, cameras, etc
        pass

# Convert 3D points to OpenGL-compatible 2D points
def gl_pts(context, v):
    return bpy_extras.view3d_utils.location_3d_to_region_2d(
        context.region,
        context.space_data.region_3d,
        v)
```

```
##### Core drawing functions #####
# Generic function for drawing text on screen
def draw_text(v, display_text, fsize, font_id=0):
    if v:
        blf.size(font_id, fsize, 72)
        blf.position(font_id, v[0], v[1], 0)
        blf.draw(font_id, display_text)
    return


# Generic function for drawing line on screen
def draw_line(v1, v2):
    if v1 and v2:
        bgl.glBegin(bgl.GL_LINES)
        bgl.glVertex2f(*v1)
        bgl.glVertex2f(*v2)
        bgl.glEnd()
    if return


##### Utilities #####


# Returns all coordinates or single coordinate of object
# Can toggle between GLOBAL and LOCAL coordinates
def coords(obj, ind=None, space='GLOBAL'):
    if obj.mode == 'EDIT':
        v = bmesh.from_edit_mesh(obj.data).verts
    elif obj.mode == 'OBJECT':
        v = obj.data.vertices

    if space == 'GLOBAL':
        if isinstance(ind, int):
            return (obj.matrix_world * v[ind].co).to_tuple()
        else:
            return [(obj.matrix_world * v.co).to_tuple() for v in v]

    elif space == 'LOCAL':
        if isinstance(ind, int):
            return (v[ind].co).to_tuple()
        else:
            return [v.co.to_tuple() for v in v]

# Returns Euclidean distance between two 3D points
def dist(x, y):
    return ((x[0] - y[0])**2 + (x[1] - y[1])**2 + (x[2] - y[2])**2)**0.5

# Returns midpoint between two 3D points
def midpoint(x, y):
    return ((x[0] + y[0]) / 2, (x[1] + y[1]) / 2, (x[2] + y[2]) / 2)
```

```python
##### Registration #####
def register():
    """Register objects inheriting bpy.types in current file and scope"""

    # bpy.utils.register_module(__name__)

    # Explicitly register objects
    bpy.utils.register_class(glrun)
    bpy.utils.register_class(glpanel)
    wm = bpy.types.WindowManager
    wm.run_opengl = bpy.props.BoolProperty(default=False)

    print("%s registration complete\n" % bl_info.get('name'))

def unregister():

    wm = bpy.context.window_manager
    p = 'run_opengl'
    if p in wm:
        del wm[p]

    # remove OpenGL data
    glrun.handle_remove(glrun, bpy.context)

    # Always unregister in reverse order to prevent error due to
    # interdependencies

    # Explicitly unregister objects
    # bpy.utils.unregister_class(glpanel)
    # bpy.utils.unregister_class(glrun)

    # Unregister objects inheriting bpy.types in current file and scope
    bpy.utils.unregister_module(__name__)
    print("%s unregister complete\n" % bl_info.get('name'))

# Only called during development with 'Text Editor -> Run Script'
# When distributed as plugin, Blender will directly call register()
if __name__ == "__main__":
    try:
        os.system('clear')
        unregister()
    except Exception as e:
        print(e)
        pass
    finally:
        register()
```

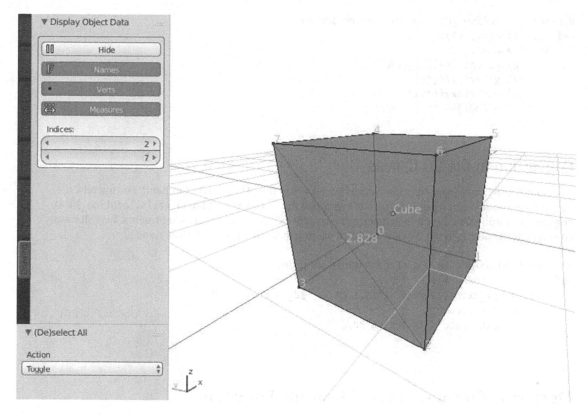

Figure 6-2. *Drawing add-on on a cube in Edit Mode*

From here, we explain the core concepts of working with bgl and blf via references to Listing 6-5. We will move from the lowest-level code (core bgl and blf) to the highest-level code (panel and handler declarations).

Drawing Lines and Text

Our goal is to draw lines and text on the canvas. The draw_text() and draw_line() functions in Listing 6-5 accomplish this by taking 2D canvas coordinates as input and passing information to bgl and blf.

```
# Generic function for drawing text on screen
def draw_text(v, display_text, fsize, font_id=0):
    if v:
        blf.size(font_id, fsize, 72)
        blf.position(font_id, v[0], v[1], 0)
        blf.draw(font_id, display_text)
    return
```

```
# Generic function for drawing line on screen
def draw_line(v1, v2):
    if v1 and v2:
        bgl.glBegin(bgl.GL_LINES)
        bgl.glVertex2f(*v1)
        bgl.glVertex2f(*v2)
        bgl.glEnd()
    return
```

Converting to the 2D Canvas

The points must be converted to the coordinate system of the 2D canvas beforehand. Fortunately, the bpy_extras module has a utility for this. We wrapped the bpy_extras.view3d_utils.location_3d_to_region_2d() utility in a function that accepts bpy.context and a 3D point as arguments. We will simply convert any 3D points to the 2D canvas before passing them to our drawing functions.

```
# Convert 3D points to OpenGL-compatible 2D points
def gl_pts(context, v):
    return bpy_extras.view3d_utils.location_3d_to_region_2d(
        context.region,
        context.space_data.region_3d,
        v
    )
```

Declaring Button-Activated Drawing Functions

The add-on will do three things:

- Label vertices of any object with their indices using label_verts().

- Display the distance and draw a line between any two vertices on an object using draw_measurement().

- Display the object's name at its origin point with draw_name().

These functions accept bpy.context, a reference to the object itself, desired indices, and color and font information to pass to draw_line() and draw_text().

■ **Note** Most of the functions performed by this add-on can be performed by starting Blender with the --debug flag or manipulating display settings of Edit Mode. This add-on is meant to serve as an example the reader can build on.

Declare Main Drawing Function

The `draw_main()` function will be executed on every frame update. The `draw_main()` function should accept `self` and `context`. It can accept any other parameters that are present in its `operator` class that we detail next, but it is encouraged that user-declared parameters are passed as `bpy.props` objects through `context`.

In each frame, the `draw_main()` function should:

- Enable OpenGL blending with `bgl.glEnable(bgl.GL_BLEND)` and set OpenGL parameters. The call to `bgl.glEnable()` allows the OpenGL scene drawn in the add-on to blend with the scene in the 3D Viewport.

- Draw each line and character.

- Disable OpenGL with `bgl.glDisable(bgl.GL_BLEND)` and reset any OpenGL parameters.

Although it is possible to not enable and disable OpenGL at every step, it is encouraged to ensure cooperation with other add-ons potentially using it.

Declaring the Operator with Handlers

The `draw_main()` function is meant to be executed at every frame update. To manage handlers in operators, we use the `@staticmethod` decorator with functions `handler_add(self, context)` and `handler_remove(self, context)`. These functions have special properties that help them nicely interact with handlers when called via `execute()`. As we have mentioned, many of the components associated with this add-on are undocumented, so we will accept them at face value. Outside of the `operator` class, we also accept lines related to `bpy.types.WindowManager` at face value.

The `glrun()` operator class in Listing 6-5 can stand in for most if not all OpenGL-enabled add-ons in Blender Python. We can typically achieve the desired result by modifying the functions outside it rather than the `operator` class itself.

Declaring the Panel with Dynamic Drawing

The panel class is fairly straightforward given our discussion of add-ons in Chapter 5. It is worth pointing out that Listing 6-5 introduces the organizational tool `self.layout.box()`, which we will discuss in Chapter 7. Also, we have introduced dynamic panels in Listing 6-5. In brief, the `draw()` class function is called on each frame update and can be modified dynamically without consequence. Chapter 7 also discusses how we can use this to make more intuitive add-ons.

Extending our bgl and blf Template

In Listing 6-5, we drew the names of objects, labeled their vertices, and drew lines and measurements from one vertex to another. Using Listing 6-5 as a template, we can easily achieve more complex and domain-specific tools.

For example, say we wanted to draw the distance from every object to every other object. This may be useful in studying the atomic structures of molecules or airline flight patterns. In both cases, we care about how close certain objects are to each other. Listing 6-6 shows a function we can add to Listing 6-5 for drawing the distance between all objects supplied to it. Figure 6-3 shows the result.

Listing 6-6. Drawing a Distance Matrix

```
# Draws the distance between the origins of each object supplied
def draw_distance_matrix(context, obs, rgb_line, rgb_label, fsize):

    N = len(obs)
    for j in range(0, N):
        for i in range(j + 1, N):
            a = obs[i].location
            b = obs[j].location
            d = dist(a, b)
            mp = midpoint(a, b)

            a_2d = gl_pts(context, a)
            b_2d = gl_pts(context, b)
            mp_2d = gl_pts(context, mp)

            bgl.glColor4f(*rgb_line)
            draw_line(a_2d, b_2d)

            bgl.glColor4f(*rgb_label)
            draw_text(mp_2d, '%.3f' % d, fsize)

# Add this to draw_main() to draw between all selected objects:
# obs = context.selected_objects
# draw_distance_matrix(context, obs, rgb_line, rgb_label, fsize)

# Add this to draw_main() to draw between all objects in scene:
# obs = context.scene.objects
# draw_distance_matrix(context, obs, rgb_line, rgb_label, fsize)
```

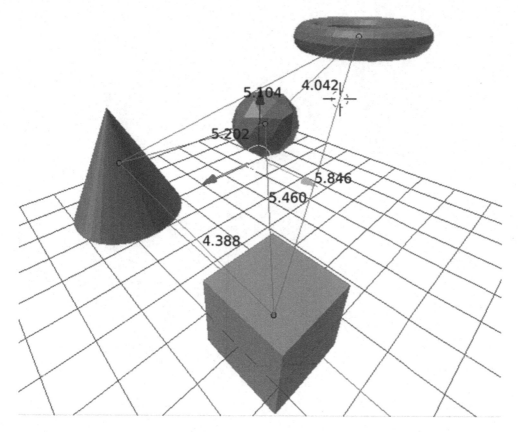

Figure 6-3. *Drawing the distance matrix*

Conclusion

In this chapter, we discussed how to use handlers, bgl and blf, to display data in real-time in the 3D Viewport. This is another tool we have at our disposal to build complete and comprehensive add-ons.

In the next chapter, we discuss advanced add-ons. We learn how to ignore the Text Editor completely and build complex add-ons directly in Blender's file tree. In addition, we study some popular open source add-ons to see how they work around many of the development challenges we have faced thus far.

CHAPTER 7

■ ■ ■

Advanced Add-On Development

This chapter discusses various topics in advanced add-on development. We conclude the chapter with an in-depth look at some of Blender's most popular add-ons.

Topics include developing in Blender's filesystem, developing outside Blender's Text Editor, organizing your add-on as a traditional Python module, advanced panel organization, data storage best practices, and submitting your add-on to Blender.

Developing in Blender's Filesystem

Up to this point, we have developed scripts and add-ons in the Blender Text Editor. We have dealt with the cumbersome task of adjusting our add-ons to work both in the Text Editor and independently as add-ons. Ultimately, manually modifying code to take it from development to deployment is an unsafe practice. We want to be certain that our code in development works exactly the same as it does in deployment.

For the development environment to mimic the deployment environment, we must develop directly in Blender's filesystem. When we refer to Blender's filesystem, we refer to the non-static application files in Blender's root directory.

First, navigate to your Blender installation. For 64-bit Blender 2.78c on Linux, it is called `blender-2.78c-linux-glibc219-x86_64`. The name varies across operating systems, so we will call this directory `blender-2.78c` throughout our discussion. The add-ons directory is located as `blender-2.78c/2.78/scripts/addons`. In this folder, we see all of our currently installed add-ons, including those that came with the Blender distribution. Some of the add-ons are single scripts, some are single-level directories, and others are complex multi-level directories.

Any valid add-on placed in this directory will appear in the Blender User Preferences. So, if we build a valid add-on from scratch, we can activate it in the User Preferences without ever opening Blender's Text Editor. We have touched on the requirements for an add-on in Chapter 5, but we have not discussed add-ons as multi-level directories. See Listing 7-1 for ASCII filetrees of various types of add-ons.

Listing 7-1. Filetrees of Various Types of Add-Ons

```
### Single Scripts     ###
### e.g. Node Wrangler ###
node_wrangler.py
```

© Chris Conlan 2017
C. Conlan, *The Blender Python API*, DOI 10.1007/978-1-4842-2802-9_7

```
### Single-level or Flat Directories ###
### e.g. Mesh Inset                   ###
mesh_inset/
|-- geom.py
|-- __init__.py
|-- model.py
|-- offset.py
'-- triquad.py


### Multi-level Directories   ###
### e.g. Rigify               ###
rigify
|-- CREDITS
|-- generate.py
|-- __init__.py
|-- metarig_menu.py
|-- metarigs
|   |-- human.py
|   |-- __init__.py
|   '-- pitchipoy_human.py
|-- README
|-- rig_lists.py
|-- rigs
|   |-- basic
|   |   |-- copy_chain.py
|   |   |-- copy.py
|   |   '-- __init__.py
|   |-- biped
|   |   |-- arm
|   |   |   |-- deform.py
|   |   |   |-- fk.py
|   |   |   |-- ik.py
|   |   |   '--__init__.py
|   |   |-- __init__.py
|   |   |-- leg
|   |   |   |-- deform.py
|   |   |   |-- fk.py
|   |   |   |-- ik.py
|   |   |   '--__init__.py
|   |   '-- limb_common.py
|   |-- finger.py
|   |-- __init__.py
|   |-- misc
|   |   |-- delta.py
|   |   '--__init__.py
|   |-- neck_short.py
|   |-- palm.py
|   |-- pitchipoy
|   |   |-- __init__.py
|   |   |-- limbs
|   |   |   |-- arm.py
```

```
|   |   |   |-- __init__.py
|   |   |   |-- leg.py
|   |   |   |-- limb_utils.py
|   |   |   |-- paw.py
|   |   |   |-- super_arm.py
|   |   |   |-- super_front_paw.py
|   |   |   |-- super_leg.py
|   |   |   |-- super_limb.py
|   |   |   |-- super_rear_paw.py
|   |   |   '-- ui.py
|   |   |-- simple_tentacle.py
|   |   |-- super_copy.py
|   |   |-- super_face.py
|   |   |-- super_finger.py
|   |   |-- super_palm.py
|   |   |-- super_torso_turbo.py
|   |   |-- super_widgets.py
|   |   '-- tentacle.py
|   '-- spine.py
|-- rig_ui_pitchipoy_template.py
|-- rig_ui_template.py
|-- ui.py
'-- utils.py
```

As we see in Listing 7-1, it is possible to build add-ons with the structure of traditional Python modules as well as single scripts and flat directories. The solution that is best for an add-on depends not so much on the size of the codebase, but on the complexity of its functions. Rigify is a great example of an add-on that necessitates multiple directories. The add-on is intended to rig (or prepare to animate) many different types of meshes. The filetree shows custom modules for legs, arms, tentacles, paws, and more, each organized into a submodule, like biped or limbs, for organization.

Creating an Add-on in the Filesystem

For this exercise, we need a text editor other than Blender's. Readers are encouraged to open their favorite IDE or text editor and create a new project. Create a directory called sandbox/ directly in Blender's add-on folder as blender-2.78c/2.78/scripts/addons/sandbox/. From there, create a file called __init__.py with the contents of Listing 7-2.

Listing 7-2. Minimal Init File for In-Filesystem Add-On

```python
bl_info = {
    "name": "Add-on Sandbox",
    "author": "Chris Conlan",
    "version": (1, 0, 0),
    "blender": (2, 78, 0),
    "location": "View3D",
    "description": "Within-filesystem Add-on Development Sandbox",
    "category": "Development",
}

def register():
    pass
```

107

```
def unregister():
    pass

# Not required and will not be called,
# but good for consistency
if __name__ == '__main__':
    register()
```

Save this file, then open Blender and navigate to **Header Menu ➤ File ➤ User Preferences ➤ Add-ons** and filter by "Development" to see our add-on, Sandbox. The result should appear as in Figure 7-1. Click the checkbox to activate our add-on, then check the terminal for errors. No news is good news, as we should see our blank add-on instantiate without errors.

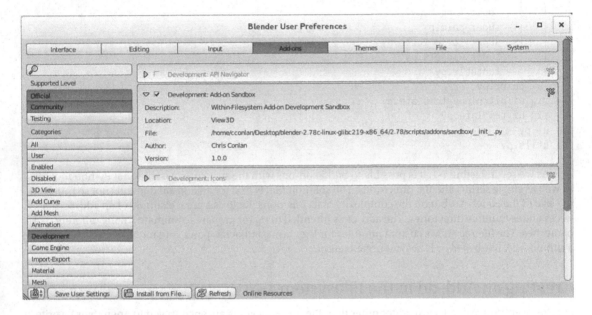

Figure 7-1. *Activating our sandbox*

After clicking the checkbox, look in `blender-2.78c/2.78/scripts/addons/sandbox/`. We see a folder called `__pycache__`, and the following filetree:

```
sandbox
|-- __init__.py
'-- __pycache__
    '-- __init__.cpython-35.pyc
```

The `__pycache__` folder is where Python stores the compiled `.py` files as `.pyc` files. Given the way Blender registers add-ons, the `*.pyc` files in the `__pycache__` directories represent the *in-memory* version of the add-on. When we click the checkbox in User Preferences, Blender makes sure that the Python source files on disk (e.g., `sandbox/__init__.py`) have not changed. If they have changed, Python will re-compile the related `__pycache__` directories and Blender will load the compiled Python into memory. Thus, while they are not strictly the same data, the compiled Python represents the current *in-memory* version of the add-on. This is why we can edit the Python source without affecting the add-on in real time.

> ■ **Note** This is not the case if Python fails to compile a `.py` file or Blender fails to reload an add-on. In this case, the add-on cannot be successfully turned on, so the in-memory version will be blank or inactive.

Using F8 to Reload Add-Ons

Now that we are editing the source of our add-on in the Blender filesystem, we can recompile the add-on to update the in-memory version. The **F8** key will reload all of the active add-ons by calling `unregister()`, recompiling the `.pyc` files if necessary, then calling `register()` on the compiled `.pyc` files. Simply press **F8** to reload *all* of the active add-ons, not just the one we may be working on. This is excellent for complex projects, especially those that depend on operators and function calls from other add-ons. In general, editing add-ons with this method is a best practice.

When we press **F8**, we should see terminal output from the `unregister()` call of the old in-memory add-on, then the `register()` function of our new in-memory add-on. If the add-on has been updated, Blender will recompile after running `unregister()` on the old add-on. If the add-on has not been updated and therefore does not require recompilation, Blender will still run the `unregister()` function.

Here is the console output for such an operation. Note that the final lines with `gc.collect()` are calls to a Python garbage collector.

```
### F8 after updating on disk... ###
### Other modules and add-ons...
reloading addon: sandbox 1491112473.307823 1491116213.6005275 /blender-2.78c/2.78/scripts/
addons/sandbox/__init__.py
module changed on disk: /blender-2.78c/2.78/scripts/addons/sandbox/__init__.py reloading...
Hello from Sandbox Registration!
gc.collect() -> 19302

### F8 without updating on disk... ###
Hello from Sandbox Unregistration!
### Other modules and add-ons...
Hello from Sandbox Registration!
gc.collect() -> 19302
```

Important Takeaway

It may seem counterintuitive, but the best practice for developing Blender add-ons is to avoid the Blender Text Editor altogether. This introduces some logistic issues concerning external text editors and IDEs, which we discuss next.

Managing Imports

Looking back to Chapter 5, Listing 5-5, the XYZ-Select add-on showed an example add-on that required modification to move from the Blender Text Editor to an add-on. Listing 7-3 shows the proper way to manage imports when editing in-filesystem. Say, for example, we had `ut.py` sitting adjacent to `__init__.py` in a flat directory. We would import it as shown in Listing 7-3.

Listing 7-3. Managing Imports While Editing In-Filesystem

```
if "bpy" in locals():
    # Runs if add-ons are being reloaded with F8
    import importlib
    importlib.reload(ut)
    print('Reloaded ut.py')
else:
    # Runs first time add-on is loaded
    from . import ut
    print('Imported ut.py')

# bpy should be imported after this block of code
import bpy
```

IDEs for In-Filesystem Development

Developing in the filesystem fundamentally changes the way we develop Blender Python scripts and add-ons, because it removes much of the accessibility and modularity we previously enjoyed in the Blender Interactive Console and Text Editor. Nonetheless, in-filesystem is the best way to develop published add-ons, and we will adjust our tools to help us with this endeavor.

Tools and features we desire in an IDE for Blender Python:

- Tab-completion or auto-complete, as typically accessed in the Interactive Console with **Ctrl+Space**

- Not creating error marks or red squiggly lines when working with bpy, bmesh, bgl, etc.

- Python code highlighting, possibly Blender-specific code highlighting, which we discuss in a few classes of options later

Lightweight (Notepad++, Gedit, and Vim)

Lightweight text editors are good for simple add-ons and scripts. In general, they have the following characteristics:

- Support syntax highlighting for Python

- Will not create error tags and red squiggly lines for Blender modules

- Do not support project management and directory browsing

- Do not have tab-completion built-in

Midweight (Sublime Text, Atom, and Spyder)

Midweight editors are a good default for programmers who do not want to spend too long configuring their IDEs. Generally, they are the same as lightweight IDEs but with project management tools. They have the following characteristics:

- Support syntax highlighting for Python

- Generally will not create error tags and red squiggly lines for Blender modules

- Have project management and directory browsing built-in

- Generally do not have tab-completion for Python built-in
- Do not have tab-completion for Blender Python built-in

Heavyweight (Eclipse PyDev, PyCharm, and NetBeans)

Heavyweight editors are good for programmers who are already used to them. They may require some configuration to work nicely with Blender Python add-ons. The option to configure is not always available. They have the following characteristics:

- Support syntax highlighting for Python
- Generally create error tags and red squiggly lines for Blender modules
- Have project management and directory browsing built-in
- Have tab-completion for Python built-in
- Do not have tab-completion for Blender Python built-in
- Can be configured to work cleanly with Blender Python

Eclipse PyDev is popular among the developer community, and developers often ask how to configure it to work with Blender Python. Eclipse in particular is very naggy about creating error markers on Blender Python module calls. Various attempts have been made to create configuration files for it, but they are not being actively maintained.

Compiling Blender as a Python Module

So far, the best catch-all solution (for all heavyweight IDEs) to lack of tab-completion is to compile Blender as a Python module. When compiled as a Python module, IDEs can descend submodules of bpy and the like to suggest corrections and enable tab-completion. We do not detail this solution here, as it is not guaranteed to work across different operating systems. Linux users interested in this solution are encouraged to research it.

Compiling Blender as a module can open up more opportunities for low-level control of your development process. Users who are able to compile Blender as a module are encouraged to check out the Sybren Stüvel's remote debugger add-on for PyCharm at his Blender add-on GitHub repo (https://github.com/sybrenstuvel/random-blender-addons). His add-on gives low-level debugging control to developers right inside PyCharm.

Summary

In the author's opinion, midweight IDEs are the best solution for Blender Python development for users who have no particular loyalty to an IDE. Many developers struggle to integrate Blender Python with heavyweight IDEs. It is not difficult to settle for a midweight IDE and refer to the Interactive Console and official documentation for API tips.

Best Practices for External Data

We shift gears here to analyze a handful of popular add-ons and critique how they handle external data. We discuss how to best deliver external data by drawing on examples from the Blender Python developer community.

In Chapter 4, we discussed the various ways in which a 3D mesh can be defined. Most notable in our discussion was the extensibility and brevity of the .obj file format in transmitting mesh, normal, and texture data between different software.

Blender Python add-ons often depend on predefined data. For example, BlenderAid's Asset Flinger allows users to easily spawn in assets from a predefined list into the scene. We discuss ways in which Asset Flinger and other add-ons get data into Blender.

Using File Interchange Formats

The Asset Flinger add-on imports meshes into Blender via .obj files. If we sift through the assets/ directory of the add-on, we see a few dozen .obj files and screenshots of them. Using interchange formats like .obj is a good way to get external data into Blender Python, because it is modular and standard to 3D artists.

This add-on allows users to extend it by adding their own .obj files. Using interchange formats is the best practice for building extensible add-ons with clear Python code. The function in Listing 7-4 is all that is required to import a .obj file into a Blender scene.

Listing 7-4. Importing OBJ Files into a Scene

```
bpy.ops.import_scene.obj(filepath=myAbsoluteFilepath)
```

As we will see, other methods of importing data can clutter your Python code and make it difficult for other developers to collaborate on it.

Using Hardcoded Python Variables

As we discussed in Chapter 4, a 3D mesh requires a minimum set of information to specify it completely, regardless of which file format is used. Some developers have used this knowledge hardcode meshes into as Python variables in their code.

Antonio Vazquez's (antonioya) Archimesh add-on allows users to create and edit architectural meshes such as walls, windows, and doors, with a custom user interface. Instead of saving these doors and windows externally in a file interchange format, he has hardcoded these meshes in Python as lists of tuples. See the Archimesh GitHub Repo at https://github.com/Antonioya/blender/blob/master/archimesh/src/ for examples of this. The tail end of many of the Python files in this repo contain hardcoded lists of tuples of vertex and face data represented by floats and integers.

This design choice is not without its motivations or consequences. In order to create rooms with arbitrary numbers of walls and windows with arbitrary numbers of panes, these Python variables are duplicated, subsetted, and transformed many times in a complex fashion. As a consequence, these objects cannot be easily substituted for one another. They are specifically designed to work with the algorithms laid out in the add-on.

The core API calls here are to bpy.data.meshes.new() and my_mesh_object.from_pydata(). The add-on creates a blank mesh, manipulates a great deal of Python data to form the object, then instantiates the mesh using the from_pydata() function on the mesh. See Listing 7-5 for a minimal example of how this add-on operates. The bottom section of Listing 7-5 shows an alternate method using bpy.ops.object.add().

Listing 7-5. Creating Meshes with from_pydata()

```
# Adapted from Antonio Vazquez's Archimesh
import bpy

# Clear scene
bpy.ops.object.mode_set(mode='OBJECT')
bpy.ops.object.select_all(action='SELECT')
bpy.ops.object.delete()
```

```
# Manipulate Python lists of vertex and face data...
# Sample here creates a triangular pyramid
myvertex = [(0.0, 0.0, 0.0), (1.0, 0.0, 0.0), (0.0, 1.0, 0.0), (0.0, 0.0, 1.0)]
myfaces = [(1, 2, 3), (1, 2, 4), (1, 3, 4), (2, 3, 4)]


#############################################################


# Option #1 - bpy.ops.object.add()
bpy.ops.object.add(type = 'MESH')
mainobject = bpy.context.object
mainmesh = mainobject.data
mainmesh.name = 'WindowMesh'
mainobject.name = 'WindowObject'


# Write the Python data to the mesh and update it
mainmesh.from_pydata(myvertex, [], myfaces)
mainmesh.update(calc_edges = True)


#############################################################


# WARNING: Known to cause crashes and segmentation faults in
# certain operating systems. Linux builds are safe.
# Option #2 - bpy.data.meshes.new()
mainmesh = bpy.data.meshes.new("WindowMesh")
mainobject = bpy.data.objects.new("WindowObject", mainmesh)


# Link the object to the scene, activate it, and select it
bpy.context.scene.objects.link(mainobject)
bpy.context.scene.objects.active = mainobject
mainobject.select = True


# Write the Python data to the mesh and update it
mainmesh.from_pydata(myvertex, [], myfaces)
mainmesh.update(calc_edges = True)


#############################################################
```

Reading through the Archimesh source code, we can see how a simple example as in Listing 7-5 can evolve into something capable of procedurally generating architectural models. Hardcoding large amounts of data may not be the most Pythonic approach to procedural generation, but it is put to good use in Archimesh. The argument can be made that the hardcoding is unnecessary and the data could be easily stored in external files, while still allowing for the use of from_pydata().

Algorithmic Manipulation of Primitives

The final method bringing mesh data into Blender is algorithmic manipulation of primitives. Primitives, in this case, refer to objects in **3D Viewport Header ➤ Add** by default. It is possible, for example, to algorithmically call Edit Mode operations on a plane to turn them into a detailed model of a window. By continually subdividing, translating, and extruding a plane, we can arrive at a complex model of a window. When we do this, the algorithm becomes the descriptor of the mesh, and it can be modified to create different variations of the mesh.

When we code algorithmic processes to create meshes, they are almost naturally modular. For example, if we created an algorithm to build a fence with 20 posts with width of 6 inches, it would naturally extend to an algorithm that builds fences with *n* posts with width *w*.

See Listing 7-6 for an example of an algorithmically generated maze. We can adjust maze_size, maze_height, fp, and buf to alter the way the maze is built. There are many points in the script that we can customize to further alter the way the maze is generated. Such is the nature of procedural generation. Parameterization comes naturally. See Figure 7-2 for an example of the output. Note that this requires the ut.py module available at http://blender.chrisconlan.com/ut.py.

Listing 7-6. Algorithmic Manipulation of a Plane, Random Maze

```
import bpy
import ut
import random

# Clear scene, must be in object mode
bpy.ops.object.select_all(action='SELECT')
bpy.ops.object.delete()

# size of maze
maze_size = 20

# height of maze
maze_height = 1.0

# Create NxN plane
bpy.ops.mesh.primitive_plane_add(radius = maze_size/ 2, location=(0, 0, 0.1))

# Subdivide and deselect mesh
bpy.ops.object.mode_set(mode='EDIT')
bpy.ops.mesh.subdivide(number_cuts=maze_size - 1)
bpy.ops.mesh.select_all(action='DESELECT')

# Set starting point
v = [-maze_size / 2, -maze_size / 2]

# Stop iterating if point strays buf away from plane
buf = 5
b = [-maze_size / 2 - buf, maze_size / 2 + buf]

# Probability of point moving forward
fp = 0.6

while b[0] <= v[0] <= b[1] and b[0] <= v[1] <= b[1]:

    # Select square in front of v
    ut.act.select_by_loc(lbound=(v[0] - 0.5, v[1] - 0.5, 0),
                         ubound=(v[0] + 1.5, v[1] + 1.5, 1),
                         select_mode='FACE', coords='GLOBAL',
                         additive=True)
```

```
    # Returns 0 or 1
    ind = random.randint(0, 1)

    # Returns -1 or 1 with probability 1 - fp or fp
    dir = (int(random.random() > 1 - fp) * 2) - 1

    # Adjusts point
    v[ind] += dir

bpy.ops.mesh.select_all(action='INVERT')
bpy.ops.mesh.extrude_region_move(TRANSFORM_OT_translate={"value": (0, 0, maze_height),
                                            "constraint_axis": (False, False, True)}
            )

bpy.ops.object.mode_set(mode = 'OBJECT')
```

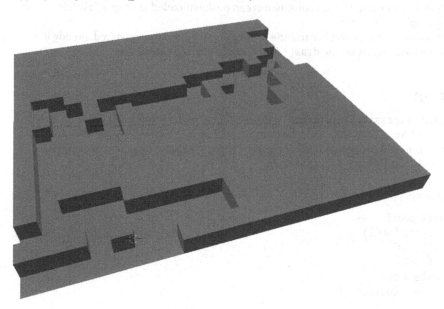

Figure 7-2. *Randomly generated maze*

Listing 7-6 uses randomness and algorithmic manipulation to generate an object. It should also be noted that algorithmic manipulation is often used to generate deterministic objects.

Summary

As a matter of best practice, it is the author's opinion that hardcoding Python variables should be avoided in favor of the other two methods: external interchange files and algorithmic manipulation. Hardcoding should be avoided mainly because external interchange files are a superior replacement for it. All of the benefits of hardcoding can be realized by reading the interchange file and holding its data within Python variables.

As a matter of practicality, it is the author's opinion that external interchange files should be used in place of algorithmic manipulation where substantial parameterization is not required. Virtually any object can be obtained with either method, but algorithmic manipulation can become unduly complicated (without benefit) in cases where parameterization is a second thought. For example, if we desire a very detailed window (1000+ vertices) and the only thing we want to parameterize is its size, algorithmically generating this window would be a poor use of development time. The preferred method here would be loading in the window from an external interchange file and resizing it using Blender's tools.

Conversely, it is easy to recognize when external interchange files will not suffice. If the original goal of the add-on is to parameterize a mesh, it is almost always best to opt for algorithmic manipulation.

Advanced Panel Creation

We conclude this chapter with a discussion of advanced panel creation. The bpy.types.Panel class has a handful of useful class methods for organizing buttons on a panel. For this discussion, we use our add-on template from Chapter 5. The version used for this discussion can be downloaded at http://blender.chrisconlan.com/addon_template.py.

To explain advanced panel customization, we use the properties and operator registered already in the template. In other words, we focus purely on the draw() function of the SimplePanel class.

Panel Organization

We have already discussed how operator() and prop() can be called to add buttons and type-specific GUI elements to the canvas, respectively. With what we have introduced thus far, readers are only able to create vertically stacked lists of buttons and properties in their panels. Listing 7-7 shows how to use organizational functions to customize panels. See Figure 7-3 for the result.

Listing 7-7. Organizing Panels

```
# Simple button in Tools panel
class SimplePanel(bpy.types.Panel)
    bl_space_type = "VIEW_3D"
    bl_region_type = "TOOLS"
    bl_category = "Simple Addon"
    bl_label = "Call Simple Operator"

    def draw(self, context):
        # Store reference to context.scene
        scn = context.scene

        # Store reference to self.layout
        lay = self.layout

        # Create box
        box = lay.box()
        box.operator("object.simple_operator", text="Print #1")
        box.prop(scn, 'encouraging_message')
```

```python
# Create another box
box = lay.box()
# Create a row within it
row = box.row()
# We can jam a few things on the same row
row.operator("object.simple_operator", text="Print #2")
row.prop(scn, 'encouraging_message')

# Create yet another box
box = lay.box()
# Create a row just for a label
row = box.row()
row.label('There is a split row below me!')
# Create a split row within it
row = box.row()
splitrow = row.split(percentage=0.2)
# Store references to each column of the split row
left_col = splitrow.column()
right_col = splitrow.column()
left_col.operator("object.simple_operator", text="Print #3")
right_col.prop(scn, 'encouraging_message')

# Throw a separator in for white space...
lay.separator()

# We can create columns within rows...
row = lay.row()
col = row.column()
col.prop(scn, 'my_int_prop')
col.prop(scn, 'my_int_prop')
col.prop(scn, 'my_int_prop')
col = row.column()
col.prop(scn, 'my_float_prop')
col.label("I'm in the middle of a column")
col.prop(scn, 'my_float_prop')

# Throw a few separators in...
lay.separator()
lay.separator()
lay.separator()

# Same as above but with boxes...
row = lay.row()
box = row.box()
box.prop(scn, 'my_int_prop')
box.label("I'm in the box, bottom left.")
box = row.box()
box.prop(scn, 'my_bool_prop')
box.operator("object.simple_operator", text="Print #4")
```

The core organizational functions of the bpy.types.Panel are box(), row(), column(), separator(), and label(). Each of these five functions can be nested within box(), row(), or column() for more granular organization. Overall, this is a very intuitive GUI development toolkit. It enables easy construction of aesthetically pleasing GUIs.

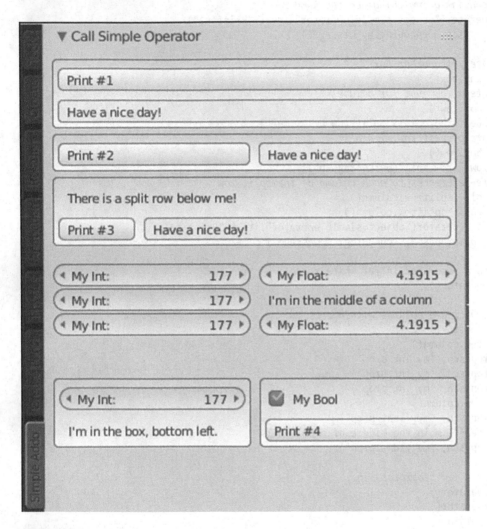

Figure 7-3. *Experimenting with panel functions*

■ **Note** Blender's GUI is built with these same tools. If you're interested in how to replicate a GUI element, right-click on it and select Edit Source to see the bpy.types.Panel class declaration for it.

Panel Icons

Looking around the Blender GUI, we notice many different icons positioned to the left of buttons. There are over 550 icons built into Blender, all of which we can use next to our own buttons. Buttons are represented by character strings that we will pass to the prop() function via the icon= argument. At the time of writing, the most comprehensive reference to the available icons is the Icons add-on that comes packaged with Blender. After activating it, press **Ctrl+F** in the Blender Text Editor to see the properties panel, where it will be located at the bottom. Listing 7-8 shows how we draw icons in the panel next to our operators. See Figure 7-4 for the result.

Listing 7-8. Panel Icons

```
class SimplePanel(bpy.types.Panel):
    bl_space_type = "VIEW_3D"
    bl_region_type = "TOOLS"
    bl_category = "Simple Addon"
    bl_label = "Call Simple Operator"

    def draw(self, context):
        # Store reference to context.scene
        scn = context.scene

        # Store reference to self.layout
        lay = self.layout

        # Create a row within it
        row = lay.row()
        row.operator("object.simple_operator", text="#1", icon='OBJECT_DATA')
        row.operator("object.simple_operator", text="#2", icon='WORLD_DATA')
        row.operator("object.simple_operator", text="#3", icon='LAMP_DATA')

        row = lay.row()
        row.operator("object.simple_operator", text="#4", icon='SOUND')
        row.operator("object.simple_operator", text="#5", icon='MATERIAL')
        row.operator("object.simple_operator", text="#6", icon='ERROR')

        row = lay.row()
        row.operator("object.simple_operator", text="#7", icon='CANCEL')
        row.operator("object.simple_operator", text="#8", icon='PLUS')
        row.operator("object.simple_operator", text="#9", icon='LOCKED')

        row = lay.row()
        row.operator("object.simple_operator", text="#10", icon='HAND')
        row.operator("object.simple_operator", text="#11", icon='QUIT')
        row.operator("object.simple_operator", text="#12", icon='GAME')

        row = lay.row()
        row.operator("object.simple_operator", text="#13", icon='PARTICLEMODE')
        row.operator("object.simple_operator", text="#14", icon='MESH_MONKEY')
        row.operator("object.simple_operator", text="#15", icon='FONT_DATA')

        row = lay.row()
        row.operator("object.simple_operator", text="#16", icon='SURFACE_NSPHERE')
```

```
        row.operator("object.simple_operator", text="#17", icon='COLOR_RED')
        row.operator("object.simple_operator", text="#18", icon='FORCE_LENNARDJONES')

        row = lay.row()
        row.operator("object.simple_operator", text="#19", icon='MODIFIER')
        row.operator("object.simple_operator", text="#20", icon='MOD_SOFT')
        row.operator("object.simple_operator", text="#21", icon='MOD_DISPLACE')

        row = lay.row()
        row.operator("object.simple_operator", text="#22", icon='IPO_CONSTANT')
        row.operator("object.simple_operator", text="#23", icon='GRID')
        row.operator("object.simple_operator", text="#24", icon='FILTER')
```

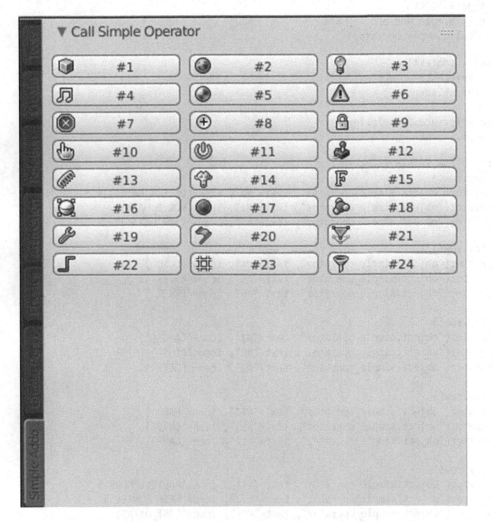

Figure 7-4. *Experimenting with panel icons*

Conclusion

Thus concludes our discussion of advanced add-ons. This guide is by no means comprehensive, as there are many places and possibilities to explore when it comes to add-on development. It is important to remember that the Blender GUI itself is built on the Python classes we have been discussing, so every functionality we see can be replicated.

The background knowledge on add-on organization in this chapter should allow readers to more easily understand the source code of other developers. Blender is an open source platform that encourages users to share code and learn from each other. Readers are encouraged to copy and modify work from other developers, then share their work for others to learn from.

The next chapter concludes this text with a treatment of texturing and rendering.

■ ■ ■

## CHAPTER 8

Textures and Rendering

So far, we have constrained our code examples to the creation of meshes and add-ons in Blender. For 3D artists and animators, the goal of 3D modeling is to make a scene come to life with rendered images and videos. Rendering in Blender Python is actually very simple, typically requiring only a single function call. To bring us to the point where we want to render our scenes, we will discuss texturing, lighting, and camera placement.

By the end of this chapter, users will be able to create automated pipelines for texturing, lighting, camera placement, and still rendering. While it is possible to render animated video with Blender Python, we will limit our discussion here to rendering still images.

Vocabulary of Textures

There are many types of textures in general, and many extra parameterized types in Blender. Our first example uses diffuse textures and normal maps to illustrate how materials function in Blender. Before we proceed, we will establish some new vocabulary about textures.

Types of Influence in Blender

While these effects are categorized as *influences* in Blender, they traditionally refer to types of textures in the broad domain of 3D modeling. Blender has its own types of textures, each of which can adopt any of these influences. See Figure 8-1 for the location of these influences in the Blender GUI. They can be found in **Properties ➤ Materials ➤ Influence**.

- *Diffuse* textures are for coloring the object. Diffuse textures can describe the color, intensity, alpha levels, and translucency of objects in Blender. To overlay an image on the face of an object, we use a diffuse color texture.

- *Shading* textures describe how the object interacts with others in the scene. If we want the object to mirror another, to emit color onto another, or spill ambient light into the scene, we specify the requisite shading properties in Blender.

- *Specular* textures describe how the object reacts to light. For example, if we supplied an image of static fuzz (as one might see on an old TV screen) as a specular texture, the light would reflect off the object like shiny grains of sand. We can fine-tune specular maps by specifying how intensely and in what direction the colors react to light.

- *Geometry* textures allows the object to affect the geometric appearance of the object. For example, if we supplied black and white stripes to a geometric map and specified a normal map, we would see 3D ridges in our model. It is important to note that these effects are realized only in rendering, not in the mesh data itself.

© Chris Conlan 2017
C. Conlan, *The Blender Python API*, DOI 10.1007/978-1-4842-2802-9_8

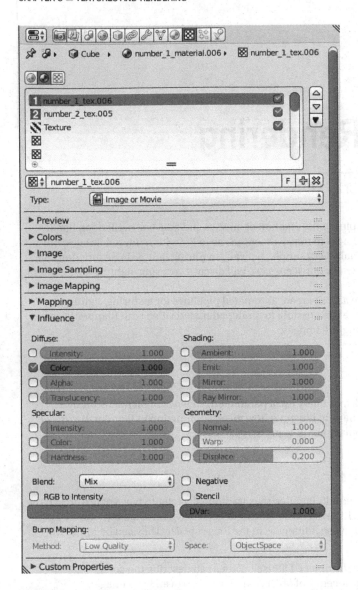

Figure 8-1. *Influences in Blender*

Types of Textures in Blender

Though we will mainly be working with image textures, Blender has numerous customizable textures we can choose from. These are selected from the **Properties ➤ Materials ➤ Type** menu shown in in Figure 8-2.

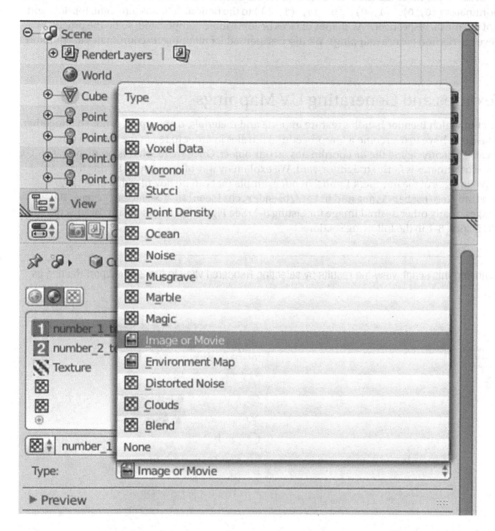

***Figure 8-2.** Texture types in Blender*

The Image and Video and Environment Map options can import image and video files. The remaining textures can be parameterized in Blender to achieve the desired result. We do not detail how to work with any of these parameterized textures specifically, as would be many dozens of parameters to discuss. Listing 8-1 explains how to work with the parameters of the Image and Video type in order to texture an object. From here, readers should be able to replicate this process for any of the remaining types using Blender's Python tooltips.

Adding and Configuring Textures

We touched on the definition of textures in Chapter 4 while discussing file interchange formats. Textures are mapped to a face in 3D space via *uv* coordinates. To map a square image as a texture to a square face of a mesh, we specify *uv* coordinates [(0, 0), (1, 0), (0, 1), (1, 1)] to the bottom-left, bottom-right, top-left, and top-right points of the mesh, respectively. As shapes of faces become more complicated, so do the processes required to achieve the desired texture mappings. We discuss method for mapping *uv* coordinates to common shapes next.

Loading Textures and Generating UV Mappings

Due to the manner in which Blender handles texture imports and materials, *uv* mapping is not an altogether straightforward task. We have to overcome a few procedural hurdles in order to reach the point in our script where we can explicitly define the *uv* coordinates on our object. Once we reach this point, precise specification of *uv* coordinates is fairly straightforward. We explain by way of example in Listing 8-1.

We use sample images of the numbers 1 and 2 in our example that can be downloaded at http://blender.chrisconlan.com/number_1.png and http://blender.chrisconlan.com/number_2.png. Readers can use these images or any other desired image for Listing 8-1. See Figure 8-4 for the result. We discuss the functions used in Listing 8-1 in the following sections.

■ **Note** After running this script, view the results by selecting Rendered view in the 3D Viewport Header, as shown in Figure 8-3.

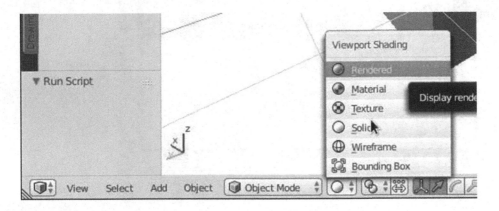

Figure 8-3. *Selecting rendered view*

Listing 8-1. Loading Textures and Generating UV Maps

```
import bpy
import bmesh
from mathutils import Color
```

```python
# Clear scene
bpy.ops.object.mode_set(mode='OBJECT')
bpy.ops.object.select_all(action='SELECT')
bpy.ops.object.delete()

# Create cube
bpy.ops.mesh.primitive_cube_add(radius = 1, location = (0, 0, 0))

bpy.ops.object.mode_set(mode = 'EDIT')

# Create material to hold textures
material_obj = bpy.data.materials.new('number_1_material')

### Begin configure the number one ###
# Path to image
imgpath = '/home/cconlan/Desktop/blender-book/ch08_pics/number_1.png'
image_obj = bpy.data.images.load(imgpath)

# Create image texture from image
texture_obj = bpy.data.textures.new('number_1_tex', type='IMAGE')
texture_obj.image = image_obj

# Add texture slot for image texture
texture_slot = material_obj.texture_slots.add()
texture_slot.texture = texture_obj

### Begin configuring the number two ###
# Path to image
imgpath = '/home/cconlan/Desktop/blender-book/ch08_pics/number_2.png'
image_obj = bpy.data.images.load(imgpath)

# Create image texture from image
texture_obj = bpy.data.textures.new('number_2_tex', type='IMAGE')
texture_obj.image = image_obj

# Add texture slot for image texture
texture_slot = material_obj.texture_slots.add()
texture_slot.texture = texture_obj

# Tone down color map, turn on and tone up normal mapping
texture_slot.diffuse_color_factor = 0.2
texture_slot.use_map_normal = True
texture_slot.normal_factor = 2.0

### Finish configuring textures ###
# Add material to current object
bpy.context.object.data.materials.append(material_obj)

### Begin configuring UV coordinates ###
bm = bmesh.from_edit_mesh(bpy.context.edit_object.data)
bm.faces.ensure_lookup_table()
```

```python
# Index of face to texture
face_ind = 0
bpy.ops.mesh.select_all(action='DESELECT')
bm.faces[face_ind].select = True

# Unwrap to instantiate uv layer
bpy.ops.uv.unwrap()

# Grab uv layer
uv_layer = bm.loops.layers.uv.active

# Begin mapping...
loop_data = bm.faces[face_ind].loops

# bottom right
uv_data = loop_data[0][uv_layer].uv
uv_data.x = 1.0
uv_data.y = 0.0

# top right
uv_data = loop_data[1][uv_layer].uv
uv_data.x = 1.0
uv_data.y = 1.0

# top left
uv_data = loop_data[2][uv_layer].uv
uv_data.x = 0.0
uv_data.y = 1.0

# bottom left
uv_data = loop_data[3][uv_layer].uv
uv_data.x = 0.0
uv_data.y = 0.0

# Change background color to white to match our example
bpy.data.worlds['World'].horizon_color = Color((1.0, 1.0, 1.0))

# Switch to object mode to add lights
bpy.ops.object.mode_set(mode='OBJECT')

# Liberally add lights
dist = 5
for side in [-1, 1]:
    for coord in [0, 1, 2]:
        loc = [0, 0, 0]
        loc[coord] = side * dist
        bpy.ops.object.lamp_add(type='POINT', location=loc)

# Switch to rendered mode to view results
```

Figure 8-4. Explicitly mapping UV coordinates

Textures Versus Materials in Blender

Texture is a broad term in 3D modeling. It can refer to diffuse textures, color textures, gradient textures, bump maps, and more. It is important to note that we can map all of these forms of textures to an object simultaneously. For example, a set of shingles on the roof of a house may require an image texture, a diffuse map, and a bump map in order to appear realistic when rendered.

Additionally, it is common for the image, diffuse map, and bump map of a real-world material to be built specifically for each other. In our shingle example, the bump map would define the ridges between the physical shingles as they appear in the image texture. The diffuse map would further define the shiny particles we typically see on roof shingles. By design, the files that represent the images and maps would not necessarily work with other files from outside the set. This is the motivation for *materials* in Blender.

A material in Blender is a collection of texture-related data. It may include any of the images and maps mentioned previously, and it may include others like normal and alpha maps. So, we must first build the material from its constituent textures, then assign the material to the object. Regardless of whether we have one or many textures comprising a material, texture data must be assigned to the material. Then, materials must be assigned to the object.

This discussion reveals the motivation behind material management in Listing 8-1. We declare and manipulate all required textures first, then we add the entire material to the object via `bpy.context.object.data.materials.append()`. From here, we can manipulate the *uv* coordinates of the entire material.

UV Coordinates and Loops

The second half of Listing 8-1 accesses a data endpoint we have not worked with previously. The *uv* coordinate data layer we aim to access is contained within a *loops* object. Loops can be thought of as 3D polygons that trace a set of vertices of a 3D object. Loops can span multiple faces, but must start and end on the same point. When loops span multiple faces, they are intended to capture a localized set of adjacent faces.

129

3D artists have access to advanced tools that help them create loops. These loops then aid them in manual assignment of *uv* coordinates. While we will not be manipulating these loops in Blender Python, it is important to understand how they work, because the loops data object lies between the mesh itself and the *uv* layer.

Fortunately, loops data objects in Blender have a 1-to-1 correspondence with `bmesh.faces[].verts[]` objects, which we are used to working with. In other words, the (*u*, *v*) coordinates accessed by `bm.faces[f].loops[v][uv_layer].uv` correspond to the (*x*, *y*, *z*) coordinates accessed by `bm.faces[f].verts[v].co` for any two integers, f and v.

It is important to note that two integers f and v may not specify a unique point in 3D space. In a default Blender 2.78c cube, as it appears in the startup file, `f:v` pairs `0:2`, `3:3`, and `4:0` all correspond to the point `(-1.0, -1.0, -1.0)` in 3D space. When the cube is textured, these *uv* coordinates will typically be unique, because they will all correspond to different parts of the texture map.

Another Note on Indexing and Cross-Compatibility

When dynamically texturing objects, we run into a problem similar to that mentioned in Chapter 3's "Note on Indexing and Cross-Compatibility". In that section, we noted that the behavior of vertex indices were *replicable but untamable,* thus justifying *selection by characteristic* as a workaround (implemented in Listing 3-13). The same concept applies here, except we must work with `bm.faces[f].verts[v].co` as opposed to just `bm.verts[v].co`.

For example, say we wanted to place a texture upright along on the *y*-axis on the top of a cube. One possible solution is to use `ut.act.select_by_loc()` from our `ut.py` toolkit to select the top face of the cube based on its location. From here, we can use `f_ind = [f.index for f in bm.faces if f.select][0]` to return the selected face index. Using the face index, we can store the face's vertices as `vert_vectors = [v.co for v in bm.faces[f_ind.verts]]` and use this information to orient our texture along the cube.

Our other option is to operate against the advice of the Chapter 3's "Note on Indexing and Cross-Compatibility" by assuming we know the location and orientation of the face vertices of an object in advance of texturing it. We can often determine this information in advance and hardcode it into our texturing scripts as we did in Listing 8-1. This is a viable option for controlled and internal use but is advised against for code that we will share with the community and that is tested for cross-version compatibility.

Based on our discussion up to this point, readers should have the tools and knowledge available to implement their desired dynamic (or non-dynamic) texturing scripts. The referenced section of Chapter 3, along with its following sections, are a strong analogue to any dynamic texturing task readers may undertake.

We now move on to discuss rendering in Blender and some of its uses.

Removing Unused Textures and Materials

We have discussed many useful functions for deleting meshes and objects in Blender. As we continually test scripts, our materials and textures data can quickly become cluttered without our realizing. Blender will rename textures to `my_texture.001`, `my_texture.002`, etc. when we neglect to delete them.

Textures and materials must *have no users* in order to be eligible for deletion. In this case, *users* refers to the number of objects that currently have it assigned. To delete textures and materials, we loop through our `bpy.data.materials` and `bpy.data.textures` datablocks and call `.remove()` on those that are not in use. See Listing 8-2 for this implementation.

Listing 8-2. Loading Textures and Generating UV Maps

```
import bpy

mats = bpy.data.materials
for dblock in mats:
    if not dblock.users:
        mats.remove(dblock)

texs = bpy.data.textures
for dblock in mats:
    if not dblock.users:
        texs.remove(dblock)
```

Rendering Using Blender Render

Using Blender's built-in rendering functions is very straightforward. We introduce and explain how to position lights and cameras in a scene, then call the rendering function to create an image. The majority of our discussion focuses on semantics and helper functions for cameras and lights.

Adding Lights

In Listing 8-1, we added six lights around our cube to make it viewable in Blender's Rendered view in the 3D Viewport. Properly using this view, and rendering in general, requires lights. Lighting is an important and large domain in 3D modeling in and of itself. In this section, we focus on Blender Python functions related to lighting rather than general practices for aesthetically pleasing lighting.

In the 3D Viewport Header, we can navigate to **Add ➤ Lamp** to select any of Blender's built-in lights. Using Python tooltips, we can see that they all rely on the function bpy.ops.object.lamp_add(), with the type= parameter determining the type of light. We have the options SUN, POINT, SPOT, HEMI, and AREA. Each of these types has its own sets of parameters to configure.

Our primary concerns when it comes to procedurally generated lighting are placement and direction. We will introduce some utilities for managing placement and direction. For example, to lazily light our entire scene, we may want to create point lights around the aggregate bounding box of the scene. Additionally, we may want to point a spotlight directly at another arbitrarily placed object. See Listing 8-3 for a list of utilities that may help with procedurally adding lights. All of the functions we declare in Listing 8-3 have been added to our toolkit ut.py, which can be downloaded at http://blender.chrisconlan.com/ut.py.

See Table 8-1 for a basic description of each type of light

Table 8-1. Types of Lights

Type	Description
Point	Emits lights equally in all directions; rotation has no effect
Spot	Emits a cone of light in a particular direction
Area	Emits light from a rectangular area; follows a Lambert distribution
Hemispheric	Similar to area, but has spherical curvature
Sun	Emits orthogonal light in a particular direction; position has no effect

Adding Cameras

Rendering a scene requires a camera. To procedurally add a camera, we must position it, adjust its direction, and modify its parameters. We will use the functions in Listing 8-3 to position and direct the cameras as well as lights.

The biggest problem we must solve when procedurally generating cameras is determining the distance and field of view such that the entire scene will be captured without appearing too small in the rendering. We will use some basic trigonometry to solve these problems.

The field of view (FoV) is a pair of two angles (θ_x, θ_y) projecting outward from a camera that defines an infinitely extending rectangular pyramid. Everything lying within this rectangular pyramid can be seen by the camera if there is nothing in front of it. To give some perspective, an iPhone 6 camera has a FoV of about $(63°, 47°)$ degrees when in landscape mode. Note that when photographers refer to FoV colloquially, they commonly refer to only the larger of the two angles.

We must understand FoV so that we can ensure the placement and calibration of the camera captures the scene we want to render.

Given a camera with FoV (θ_x, θ_y) centered along and facing a scene with bounding box of height h and width w, the distance from the scene d required to capture the scene is $max(d_x, d_y)$. For this discussion, d_x and d_y represent the requisite distance to capture the scene along the horizontal and vertical dimensions, respectively. See Figure 8-5 for a visual representation. Using basic trigonometry, we arrive at

$$d_x = \frac{w}{2}cot(\frac{\theta_x}{2})$$

$$d_y = \frac{h}{2}cot(\frac{\theta_y}{2})$$

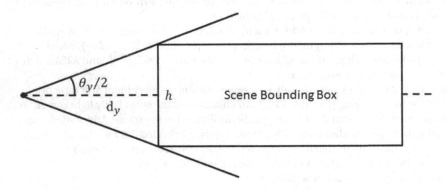

Figure 8-5. *Field of view along the y-axis*

This only accounts for the simple case where the camera is pointing along the *x*- or *y*-axis, but it will suffice for our purposes. In Listing 8-4, we use utility functions established previously to direct the camera such that it can render the entire visible scene.

Listing 8-3. Utilities for Lights and Cameras

```
# Point a light or camera at a location specified by "target"
def point_at(ob, target):
    ob_loc = ob.location
    dir_vec = target - ob.location
    ob.rotation_euler = dir_vec.to_track_quat('-Z', 'Y').to_euler()
```

```
# Return the aggregate bounding box of all meshes in a scene
def scene_bounding_box():

    # Get names of all meshes
    mesh_names = [v.name for v in bpy.context.scene.objects if v.type == 'MESH']

    # Save an initial value
    # Save as list for single-entry modification
    co = coords(mesh_names[0])[0]
    bb_max = [co[0], co[1], co[2]]
    bb_min = [co[0], co[1], co[2]]

    # Test and store maxima and minima
    for i in range(0, len(mesh_names)):
        co = coords(mesh_names[i])
        for j in range(0, len(co)):
            for k in range(0, 3):
                if co[j][k] > bb_max[k]:
                    bb_max[k] = co[j][k]
                if co[j][k] < bb_min[k]:
                    bb_min[k] = co[j][k]

    # Convert to tuples
    bb_max = (bb_max[0], bb_max[1], bb_max[2])
    bb_min = (bb_min[0], bb_min[1], bb_min[2])

    return [bb_min, bb_max]
```

Rendering an Image

Rendering is the process of computing high-resolution imagery and video given 3D data. Rendering is not instantaneous. While the 3D Viewport in Blender seems to move fluidly as we translate and rotate the camera, rendering can take a considerable amount of time. The 3D Viewport *is* an instantaneous rendering of the 3D data, but it does not represent the same level of quality or definition as a traditional rendering.

In Listing 8-4, we render the output of Listing 8-1 using both Blender Render and OpenGL render. This example assumes positions the camera to point upward along the x-axis at the median of the scene, from the yz-median of the scene, such that it will capture the whole scene. We use the equations discussed previously to accomplish this. Recall that these equations assume the simple case that we are pointing the camera along an axis.

The resulting rendering captures the object squarely within the frame. See Figure 8-6 for the Blender Render of the cube created in Listing 8-1. For the Blender Render, the scene's camera is used as the rendering camera. This is why it is important to know how to set the camera's position procedurally. If we want to loop through and render many scenes, we need to be confident that the scene will be captured within the frame.

Figure 8-6. *Blender Render*

We can also render a snapshot of the 3D Viewport using OpenGL render. This will capture basic features of the scene similar to how we see the 3D Viewport in Object Mode with Solid view. See Figure 8-7 for the result. Note that we can see both the lights and camera, but not the materials, in this view. When we call `bpy.ops.render.opengl()`, setting `view_context` = `True` will cause Blender to use the 3D Viewport camera (the user's view) rather than the scene camera.

Listing 8-4. Rendering Using Blender Render and OpenGL Render

```
### Assumes output of Listing 8-1 is in scene at runtime ###

import bpy
import bmesh
import ut

from math import pi, tan
from mathutils import Vector

# Get scene's bounding box (meshes only)
bbox = ut.scene_bounding_box()

# Calculate median of bounding box
bbox_med = ( (bbox[0][0] + bbox[1][0])/2,
             (bbox[0][1] + bbox[1][1])/2,
             (bbox[0][2] + bbox[1][2])/2 )

# Calculate size of bounding box
bbox_size = ( (bbox[1][0] - bbox[0][0]),
              (bbox[1][1] - bbox[0][1]),
              (bbox[1][2] - bbox[0][2]) )
```

```python
# Add camera to scene
bpy.ops.object.camera_add(location=(0, 0, 0), rotation=(0, 0, 0))
camera_obj = bpy.context.object
camera_obj.name = 'Camera_1'

# Required for us to manipulate FoV as angles
camera_obj.data.lens_unit = 'FOV'

# Set image resolution in pixels
# Output will be half the pixelage set here
scn = bpy.context.scene
scn.render.resolution_x = 1800
scn.render.resolution_y = 1200

# Compute FoV angles
aspect_ratio = scn.render.resolution_x / scn.render.resolution_y

if aspect_ratio > 1:
    camera_angle_x = camera_obj.data.angle
    camera_angle_y = camera_angle_x / aspect_ratio
else:
    camera_angle_y = camera_obj.data.angle
    camera_angle_x = camera_angle_y * aspect_ratio

# Set the scene's camera to our new camera
scn.camera = camera_obj

# Determine the distance to move the camera away from the scene
camera_dist_x = (bbox_size[1]/2) * (tan(camera_angle_x / 2) ** -1)
camera_dist_y = (bbox_size[2]/2) * (tan(camera_angle_y / 2) ** -1)
camera_dist = max(camera_dist_x, camera_dist_y)

# Multiply the distance by an arbitrary buffer
camera_buffer = 1.10
camera_dist *= camera_buffer

# Position the camera to point up the x-axis
camera_loc = (bbox[0][1] - camera_dist, bbox_med[1], bbox_med[2])

# Set new location and point camera at median of scene
camera_obj.location = camera_loc
ut.point_at(camera_obj, Vector(bbox_med))

# Set render path
render_path = '/home/cconlan/Desktop/blender_render.png'
bpy.data.scenes['Scene'].render.filepath = render_path

# Render using Blender Render
bpy.ops.render.render( write_still = True )
```

```
# Set render path
render_path = '/home/cconlan/Desktop/opengl_render.png'
bpy.data.scenes['Scene'].render.filepath = render_path

# Render 3D viewport using OpenGL render
bpy.ops.render.opengl( write_still = True , view_context = True )
```

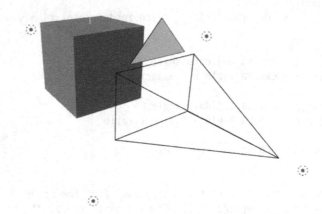

Figure 8-7. *OpenGL rendering*

Conclusion

This chapter concludes our discussion of the Blender Python API. Even with its many examples, this text is not a comprehensive guide. This is a testament to the complexity and modularity of Blender more than anything else. Blender can be edited, tweaked, customized, and expanded using the Python API. The author of this book and the dedicated professionals that assisted in its development hope that this knowledge helps encourages research and development in the Blender community.

Index

A

Abstraction, 16
Add-on development
    advanced panel creations (*see* Advanced panel creation)
    algorithmic manipulation of primitives, 113–115
    bl_info dictionary, 69–70
    bpy.types.Operator, 70–71
    deployment and sharing, 79–81, 83
    distribution, 85
    EnumProperty, 85
    hardcoded Python variables, 112–113
    IDEs, 110–111
    imports, 110
    init file, 107–108
    interchange formats, 112
    panels and class inheritance, 71–72
    poll() classmethod, 84
    register() and unregister(), 72–74, 109
    scene properties and bpy.props, 74–79
    template, 65–68
    types, 105–106
Advanced panel creation
    organizational functions, 116–118
    panel icons, 119–120
Application programming interface (API), 71

B, C

bgl and blf modules
    distance matrix, 102
    handler (*see* Handlers)
bmesh module
    3D object, 30
    Edit Mode (*see* Edit Mode Transformations)
    global and local coordinates, 35–37
    indexing and cross-compatibility, 34
    objects, 29
    random shape growth, 40–42
    selecting pieces, 37–38
    transforming pieces, 39

bpy module
    abstraction, 16
    activation, 14–15
    app, 12
    context, 11
    data, 12
    multivariate data visualization (*see* Multivariate data)
    objects, 11
    path, 12
    props, 12
    pseudo-circular referencing, 16
    selection, 13–14
    specification, 15–16
    transformations, 17–19
    types, 12
    utils, 12

D

Default Blender interface
    command line, 7
    dual-screen development, 6
    3D Viewport, 3
    header, 3
    property, 3
    Python, 8
    scripting (*see* Scripting interface)
    Timeline, 3
    Tool Properties, 3
    Tool Shelf, 3
3D modeling
    .blend, 48
    concentric normals, 56–59
    coplanar surfaces, 52–53
    cube, 48
    face vertices, 53–55
    flipped normals, 60–61
    naive specification, 48–50
    .obj and .mtl, 45–46
    PLY, 47
    primitives, 55

© Chris Conlan 2017
C. Conlan, *The Blender Python API*, DOI 10.1007/978-1-4842-2802-9

Get the eBook for only $5!

Why limit yourself?

With most of our titles available in both PDF and ePUB format, you can access your content wherever and however you wish—on your PC, phone, tablet, or reader.

Since you've purchased this print book, we are happy to offer you the eBook for just $5.

To learn more, go to http://www.apress.com/companion or contact support@apress.com.

Apress®

Printed in the United States
By Bookmasters